Perennial Ceremony

Perennial Ceremony

Lessons and Gifts from a Dakota Garden

TERESA PETERSON

University of Minnesota Press

Minneapolis

London

A note from the author: The Dakota language has dialect differences and various ways to convey a thought, depending on band and community, as well as multiple Dakota orthographies. All are fine. I do my best to honor my language teachers and Pejuhutazizi, the place I call home.

The author and the University of Minnesota Press thank Raine Cloud for her help with the Dakota language in this book.

Published by the University of Minnesota Press
111 Third Avenue South, Suite 290
Minneapolis, MN 55401-2520
http://www.upress.umn.edu

ISBN 978-1-5179-1702-9 (hc)
ISBN 978-1-5179-1721-0 (pb)

Library of Congress record available at https://lccn.loc.gov/2024002383

Printed in the United States of America on acid-free paper

The University of Minnesota is an equal-opportunity educator and employer.

30 29 28 27 26 25 24   10 9 8 7 6 5 4 3 2 1

Tokata wicoicaġe kiŋ ohna woyuonihaŋ uŋpi

▼

In dedication for all the generations to come

Contents

EMBRACE THE CURVE

Roads, driveways, fields of corn blur past me.
My eyes dart from fence lines and rows of pines defining
    homesteads and outlining held acreage.
The lines measure and count. They keep in and keep out.

Parallel lines, vertical lines, and cross points invisibly mapping
    across Mother Earth.
Boundary lines held in our imaginary minds, corral decisions and
    maintain uninspired deeds.

Returning home, I search for the expansive arc, the infinite
    circles, the curve of helices.
The circular heads of the late summer sunflowers bend ever so
    slightly, greeting me with a curtsy.
The taut skins wrapped around Joe's oxhearts, the Hungarian
    hearts, and the Amish pastes blush with their fullness.

Our Good Mother Stallard makes her way climbing the spiral
    staircase toward heaven,
her viny limbs weaving in and out to support herself, knowing a
    straight line will not do.

Late in the day, when the sun radiates a final burst of fiery
    orange and waves of fuchsia
I greet Norah's melody with a knowing smile as she invites me
    to come away with her
My hip sways and lures my mate to turn me on
His arms encircle the still fullness of my belly that formerly held
    three of our babes
And I grasp that our love is surely not a line but an infinite,
    ever-expanding circle that will live beyond our time.

Introduction
Gardening Is Ceremony

"Gardening is ceremony. Gardening is ceremony." I continued to repeat this mantra over and over while I spent hours and days weeding back my garden. At times my heart and spirit professed the sacred words with a deep reverence for the land, *Dakota land*, as I sat contentedly, tailbone grounded to the earth. Other times as I crawled on hands and knees it emerged as a question, "Is gardening ceremony?" I made my way across the 50-by-120-foot space, removing an abundance of tall patches of crabgrass, bull thistle, Canadian thistle, redroot pigweed, ragweed, and horseweed, some waist high. There were entanglements of wild buckwheat and purslane and bushy overgrown lambsquarters and black nightshade dotted throughout. Some I found growing right next to a tomato or pepper plant, as if in competition. I know that many of the "weeds" I was pulling are beneficial, and I could have used them for medicine or nutritious eating. But now they were taking up the nutrients, moisture, and, in some cases, sunlight from the plants I had intended to grow.

The garden has always been a space for me to work through my own everyday problems or to reflect on issues too big for me to solve. The winds seem to whisper a poignant thought, perspective is found by scanning the expansive blue sky, or a winged relative sings "all is well." Sometimes an explication pushes up to the surface, yet it is firmly rooted in the knowing clarity that indicates it is the right solution, just as a seed coat breaks open and a seedling emerges yet underneath, the roots firmly setting and spreading. The garden is a place of refuge and a sanctuary space for me. Yet this is not how I wanted to spend hot days in late July after my return. Besides harvesting a few earlier crops, this stretch of the growing season ought to be dedicated to picking the bounty of green beans, zucchinis, and raspberries. This is the time when the tomato plants are kicking out green tomatoes and the three sisters (corn, beans, and squash) are robust and show sure signs of a future harvest. Through trial and error, I have learned it is more beneficial and efficient when we direct our efforts to weeding and nurturing seedlings *earlier* in the season rather than later. When it's 90 and 100 degrees, we want to spend minimal energy in removing a "weed" here and there. But that doesn't mean we can walk away for two weeks and not expect mayhem upon return.

While I admit I have never been gone that long, I am quite sure I gave explicit directions and reminders to my fellow family gardeners before and during my two-week leave. I had even ensured that every weed was out of the garden before my departure to Oahu in July 2012. Now I was sure that Creator, karma, fate, or whatever you want to call it was challenging the enlightenment gained during my retreat to paradise.

Sometimes those profound understandings, such as *gardening is ceremony*, can occur only when you step outside your everyday habitat. I had to travel four thousand miles from my garden sanctuary to understand that I can have a spiritual experience anywhere—in my garden and even in an ocean. My spiritual connections do not have to be held in a building, be prescribed, or, much less, motivated by guilt. My garden that sits overlooking the bluff of the Mni Sota River valley provides me a place of worship and spiritual connection, just as it has for my Dakota and Indigenous ancestors for time immemorial. And similar to those of Dakota *wiŋyaŋ* (women) from long ago, my garden extends beyond the dedicated soil I have worked up for planting. For example, the front yard holds nine towering maple trees that get tapped annually in the early spring to cook down into sweet, sticky syrup. Past the garden shed is a blackberry patch among the apple and pear trees. The backyard and into the woods provide an abundance of edibles too—wild plums, grapes, and gooseberries. Beyond the confines of our lands are gathering and foraging opportunities for medicines and foods that feed our physical and spiritual needs. *Ina Maka* (Mother Earth), whether land, water, plant, or animal nations, all provide a cornucopia of perennial ceremony, lessons and gifts for my body, mind, and soul. As I continued to tend to the arduous task of weeding and nurturing my own slice of paradise, these thoughts permeated my being, knowing that gardening *is* ceremony.

SCANNING THE DARKNESS, the tiny light that comes before the dawn peered out from the horizon. At a beach in Oahu, my toes sank into the sand and I gazed at the ocean directly in front of us—I was ready for Uncle Hauʻoli and his family to guide us through the instructions again, reiterating what he told us the night before. My classmates and I joined hands in one long line, our sleepy brains listening intently to the song. Each of us slowly joined in the repeated verses, then entered the cool Pacific waters.

As the sun's brilliance rose over the ocean and through the eastern sky, *E ala ē* became a soothing reverberation that helped clear any lingering drowsiness and shifted me into a spiritual and meditative state. After moving farther out and creating my own sacred space in the vast waters, I dug my toes in the sand to gain a footing between the laps of waves. A realization washed over me of solo wonderment in that each of us defines and constructs our own spiritual connection to *all that is.* Salty water lapped at my thighs as I pondered the teachings from our generous hosts. One teaching included the connection of our spiritual essence to multiple relationships and spaces in time, all contained through portals within our bodily vessel. The fontanelle—the once-soft spot on the top of our heads as infants—connects to our ancestors and our past, the navel links us to our children and family and the present, and our genitals connect us to our grandchildren and future generations. This teaching reminded me of our own Dakota teaching of seven generations past and seven generations into the future and that our present actions ought to reflect that. I tried to make this connection to the Christian teachings of my childhood. Unsuccessful, I prayed silently to be able to release the internal struggle I had for years between Christian doctrine and Native traditions. I reflected on the beautiful ceremony we were collectively partaking in and its ability to hold sacred communion with Creator at an individual intimate level, yet recognizing we are just one small part of an interconnected whole. I recognized this same feeling of intimacy from precious memories of my childhood on the farm. There was the simple joy of riding in a sun-faded red gravity box filled to the top with oats, me alongside my brother, grasshoppers, and the blue sky above; the wonderment in watching piglet after piglet come into the world—while I wiped the birthing goop from their noses and mouths and placed them under the heat lamp near their mama; walking trails along the back grove and hearing the welcoming spring sounds of red-winged blackbirds and the search for cattails and pussy willows in the ditches alongside quiet gravel roads; pocketed stillness felt while ice-skating on an isolated pond or inside a frozen fort we built out of heaps of snow; and even revered sadness from the interconnectedness understood from a piglet's death or that of a barn kitten. These sacred moments resurfaced while the profundity of this intimate moment flooded my cells—as this, too, was a communion with all of creation. Creator, God, *Wakaŋ Taŋka* was everywhere and here for everyone, in any moment, at any time. This understanding called to me—to find and shape my own relationship with creation instead of relying upon prescribed doctrine.

The seawaters seemed to carry away the guilt I habitually carried, a characteristic I attribute to a strict religious upbringing. I decided then and there that I would commit to living a spiritual life that felt right for *me.* I would be self-vigilant in ensuring my spiritual motivations were mine, just as participating in this very sunrise ceremony was my choice and not one borne out of pressure.

After some time passed, I was ready to release my lei. I would leave all my entreaties and thoughts, burdens and requests made

On the farm in 1977.

in this moment and of those that surfaced the night before while our group prepared and made our leis. I removed the lei from around my neck and held the woven ti leaves tight with both hands. Letting go was difficult. I questioned if I had covered everything. Did I make the right requests? I paused. Doubts were trying to creep in between me and my lei. Slowly, the ends of my lip curled up. I recognized this hesitation to be my habit of caution and control—my fear of letting go. I didn't need to figure it out. That was not my responsibility. The exchange of faith, the intimate communion with Creator and *all that is* contained my humble pleadings and gifts of gratitude. All I needed to do was let go. Just then, an overwhelming feeling of unconditional love seemed to put the release into motion and filled the imaginary space between all that I was holding and letting go.

My private communion concluded with a salty cleansing. I dunked my head three times as had been shared, symbolizing the connection between my ancestors, family, and coming descendants. For a few brief moments I stood there, liberation washing over me. My mind filled with a desire to hold on to this level of peace and serenity in my life. I reflected on the teachings and ceremonies of Christianity and those from Dakota traditions. I considered my bicultural identity and spirituality and the way they manifest in my life. Some aspects of the rigid religious dogma I was raised with have been difficult to reconcile with the Dakota practices shared and learned along the way, as well as the spiritual insights gained by being in communion with nature. The internal struggle reminded me of something Louise Erdrich wrote in *The Antelope Wife*: "You make a person from a German and an Indian, for instance, and you're creating a two-souled warrior always fighting with themselves." Which shall I claim as a daily practice tomorrow and the days to follow? Finally, relieved, I no longer felt chained to the perpetual back-and-forth of either this or that, that had consumed much of my adult life. I no longer felt the heavy burden of guilt that accompanied me daily. Nor did I feel I was betraying one practice, belief, or faith for the other. For that moment in time, I let go of any remaining concern. The only commitment made was to no longer do things because I should or ought to. Instead, I would reclaim a spiritual health that is nurturing, reciprocal, and fulfilling.

The leis of my classmates began gently bobbing past me—their prayers and needs also being carried east. I rejoined the ceremonial group, and we closed the morning's sacred journey of making things right for the day. *E ala ē.* I welcomed the sun and the light now that I had made room for newness.

My mind and spirit have relived that transformational moment many times since. That spiritual experience and graduate school itself was a pivotal time in my life. It became the basis for answering core questions about my cultural identity and the lack of belongingness I often felt in our othering society. Subsequently, it also fueled the research to fulfill my doctoral requirements. I was part of an Indigenous Education cohort through the University of Minnesota Duluth, with about half of us Native. It was in 2012, when our second summer session was held, and we would spend two weeks together. Our courses included Research Design, Teaching and Learning in Systems Context, and Doctoral Seminar. The best part was that classes were held in Oahu, Hawaii, while we stayed at the Hawaiʻi Pacific University Hawaii Loa Campus. Our mornings were spent with local Hawaiians supporting grassroots efforts in language immersion education, ecological restoration, and cultural revitalization. They called us by kinship terms, and I was seen as a kindred sister to our Hawaiian relatives. We helped our relatives replant taro plants, remove invasive plants, and learned about traditional canoeing through star navigation. We toured sacred spaces, climbed mountains to find freshwater springs, and learned of Hawaiian resistance to the all-too-familiar colonization of Indigenous peoples and land. During the afternoons we held class with Indigenous instructors and guest scholars. This is and remains a rare privilege. I shall never forget our mentors and their unique and passionate styles of teaching and sharing—Dr. Tom Peacock, Anishinaabe; Dr. Brian McGinnis, Anishinaabe; Dr. Peter Hanohano, Hawaiian; and Dr. Manulani Aluli Meyer, Hawaiian.

The evenings were relegated to writing papers and completing assignments for the non-procrastinators. While reluctant at times, I was glad to have returned home without any incompletes, although I missed some of the cultural and social activities. But there was an activity one evening for which I chose to leave my dorm room. It was lei making and the beginning of the next day's sunrise ceremony. Uncle Hauʻoli, as we called him out of respect and honor, along with his family had gathered enough lāʻī or ti leaves for each of us to prepare and braid leis for the ceremony. I recall being frustrated, not getting the technique down, yet not wanting to ask for help. But in the end, I meekly asked Auntie for assistance in order to complete the process before nighttime.

Getting up so early that morning, in the dark, was difficult. Yet, I was intrigued with the idea that we would be in ceremony at the beach. I am grateful for the humble ritual—*To Arise*—that connected me so simply and profoundly to the rising of the sun and am forever changed. The ceremony that awakened the light in me brought me to ponder the mindfulness of my gardening and gathering practices. It seemed the observational stance I am inclined to, and it became an opportunity to just be. Being out on

the land we call home offers me a neutral space where dichoto-
mies are blurred and are no longer in contradiction. The planting and growing spaces and the foraging and healing landscapes
that overlook the wide Mni Sota River valley provide me spiritual
sanctuary. I continue to cultivate this way of life, as it heals, nurtures, and sustains my spirit, body, and mind. My affinity to the
garden is akin to Mary Oliver's relationship to the woods: "For me
the door to the woods is the door to the temple" (*Upstream*, page
154). As I commune with the land beneath my feet, the homelands of my Dakota people, I have come to understand that *gardening is ceremony.*

Dakota elder and retired Episcopal minister John Robertson
once shared with me, "Your culture and traditions are reflected in
the way that you live." He rhetorically asked me, "What are your
rituals, your ceremonies? What do you do when you wake up?
What do you do to celebrate the week?" According to *Merriam-
Webster's Collegiate Dictionary,* eleventh edition, *caerimonia,* the
Latin word for "ceremony," is defined as "a formal act or series
of acts prescribed by ritual, protocol, or convention." As I reflect
upon the sunrise ceremony and my return from the place of *ha*
(breath), *wai* (fresh water), and *ea* (spirit), I notice the importance
of similar concepts in our own Dakota language, *ni, mni,* and *naġi.*
The exchange of breath, water, and spirit is ever present in my protocols and rituals of growing, foraging, preparing, and preserving
sustenance. These daily, weekly, and seasonal practices and rituals
make up a year-round ceremony.

OVER THE YEARS, seeds of thought emerged as I worked in the
garden, tended to plants, and cared for the land. Writing became
the soil from which grew a collection of seasonal reflections from
my heart and mind, sensory observations, and spiritual experiences as a gardener and lover of the land. What emerged through
the help of breath, water, and spirit—and, of course, a little weeding—is four chapters: *Wetu* (Spring), *Bdoketu* (Summer), *Ptaṇyetu*
(Fall), and *Waniyetu* (Winter). Sections within each chapter are
titled by concepts or expressions of ceremony that I have expe-

rienced, including Christian ceremonies of baptism, marriage, and communion; Dakota traditional practices of *inipi* (sweat lodge), *wicahnakapi* (funeral), and *azidya* (smudge); or *E ala ē*, the beautiful sunrise ceremony our Hawaiian relatives held for me and my fellow scholars; and even those daily rites I have made up, such as the salutation to the eastern sky off my deck each morning whether in the rain, snow, or dark. After all, as Shawn Wilson writes in *Research Is Ceremony,* "The purpose of any ceremony is to build stronger relationships or bridge the distance between aspects of our cosmos and ourselves." Yet, the countless ceremonial and spiritual attributes that provide an abundance of healing and wellness are informed by my year-round gardening rites. These heavenly and earthly interludes are captured through creative literary vignettes, educational text, poetry, and even a few recipes.

I invite you to join me in a journey across four Dakota seasons— *Wetu,* the time of blood or when things grow; *Bdoketu,* the time of the potato; *Ptaŋyetu,* the time of the otter; and *Waniyetu,* the time when the snow lives. As a gardener, seasons direct my life more often than a calendar, and I am attentive to the subtle changes throughout the year. As a reader, I ask you to drop the linear mindset we have been trained to have through our colonial education systems. My writing does not necessarily track chronologically, and, in fact, it may be important to know that I wrote this collection over three years. The recipes included are those commonly enjoyed at our table, each containing several ingredients we grew in our garden or foraged and harvested from surrounding lands. I include the recipes to encourage you as the reader and current or aspiring gardener and forager to try them out—adjusting the recipe as you so desire.

As I sit here and write this, we are experiencing a summerlike spring after a long, cold winter. Initially delayed, everything spring is now flourishing. Earlier, I walked past the row of various lilacs, stopping to smell each one—the dark-purple ones, a pink one, a white, and the standard lavender-colored one, each with a distinct fragrance. The honeysuckle bushes along the wooded trails smell divine, and soon our tables will hold vases full of fragrant peonies. Toward the garden, the apple and pear trees just shed their blossoms, and I spotted two blossoms in the strawberry patch. We are adding fresh chives to several dishes and picking asparagus daily. We are snacking on muffins from the first cutting of rhubarb and drinking cold *ceyaka wahpe* (mint tea) made with apple mint, spearmint, and peppermint. With the windows open, I hear the trilling sounds of a Cope's gray treefrog, who must have made a home near our back porch. I take a moment to wonder if its home is in the shady patch of ferns below or above in the canopy of the vining wisteria—and perhaps it traverses both depending upon the day's heat. Either way, it makes me happy, remembering that frogs are a sign of environmental health. I could just keep on writing, as each day brings something new or different during this time of growth.

Through this collection of writing, I have come to understand that ceremony is nestled within the daily and seasonal activities, and I began reflecting upon all the aspects that this way of life intersects with the tenets of sacred rites, rituals, and observations. These tenets (principles or beliefs) are not an exhaustive list but rather a mere recollection drawn from my own perennial odyssey. These principles became the thematic listing or sections within each season. Overlapping, shortened, or extended seasons, and global warming, influence what, when, and how we grow and gather food, and our adaptability is needed now more than ever. More importantly, climate change and its impact on Mother Earth calls us to examine our relationships; all our relationships—with our neighbors, the animals and plants, the water, and land. It can simply begin with observation, slowing down, and asking ourselves, *What is our relationship to the land?*

Wetu

WETU AHI

Morning star
Shining bright before the mother
    of all stars
lights my prayer of dawn, as I rise.

Listening for her
as if eavesdropping.
Not hearing a sound
more of a stirring usually felt
    deep in the night.
An opening, perhaps
revealing a flow deep within her.

A flight of gossip
scratches my curiosity.
The path beckons my step
left, right, left.
Sing songs replaced with silence.
I stop, with held breath
Drip.
Silence.
A suspended drop, her sweetness
    hanging.
Finally plunging.

A wide-eyed morning
I listen, head tilted
I feel the curl before a knowing
    smile.
Crunch-smoosh. Crunch.
Refrained steps hold a stillness,
as steam escapes my cradled
    breath.
Assuredly, my belly rises.
Coolness fills my nostrils, with
    insides refreshed.
In and out, I take her in.

He collects her fresh sweetness
generosity overflowing
some as vapor rising from the
    cracks.
Beaks open
branches stretch wide
all taking her in.
In and out
my chest rises, holds then falls.
Long awaited by all.
Spring arrives.

Spring
The Time of Blood

▲▲▲

AN AWAKENING

Kitaŋ̇! Wetu ahi. (Finally! Spring has arrived.) Spring is making its way here in Mni Sota Makoce (the Land of Cloudy Waters), and *Waziya* (Old Man Winter) is finally heading north. It is during this transitional time we can gather the sweet sap that the maples so willingly give up. Good thing we have the weather app on our phones so that we know when the time is right. Aye—as if! Before the age of technology, we would have perhaps consulted the *Farmer's Almanac* or maybe, just intuitively known it was time to tap the maple trees. Yet, there are other signs if one is willing to pay attention. For example, just this weekend, I heard honkers across the road. There is a little depression in the landscape, a small wetland, and an ideal place for waterfowl to take a rest. Too, I spotted a skunk shuffling in a ditch. While the skunks do not necessarily hibernate, they are more inactive during the bitter cold and snowy weather. Their body temperatures and heart rates slow, and they drift off into a deep sleep called torpor. Yep, I definitely associate the frequent smell of skunk with a sign of spring.

During early spring, the warming temperatures during the day and back to freezing temperatures at night are what provide the right conditions for the tree's stored sap to flow up the trunk and back down to the roots. This back-and-forth aligns with this transitional period of not quite spring, yet not finished with winter.

Conversely, last fall when our Autumn Blazes were dropping their scarlet leaves, they began storing extra energy into a concentrated sucrose in their roots. It is similar to our own biological process of additional fuel (too much food) that is stored as fat reserves. And the cycle prior to that, during the summer, light is being captured through the leaves and converted into starch. This starch supports the life and growth of the tree, a magical process called photosynthesis. Some of you might remember this term from your science class. Ideal conditions for sap to flow are when temperatures rise above and below freezing—for example, 40s during the day and 20s at night. It is this back-and-forth that creates pressure within for sap to flow down the tree due to gravity or out through a broken branch. Tapping trees takes advantage of the traveling energy, by capturing some of the life-giving sap.

Each year, my partner, Jason, gathers sap from the trees so I can make syrup. Jason (or Jay, as he prefers) is Dakota and from the same small rez as me. Both of his parents are Dakota and from the Sisseton Wahpeton Oyate. His mother grew up on the Lake Traverse Reservation—the Ḣeipa District, to be precise. His father grew up in the Upper Sioux Community, the related and original eastern Dakota lands in Minnesota. Jay was born over in Sisseton but grew up in both communities after his parents split up. Later he made his permanent home at Upper Sioux when he and his dad returned from a stint on the Fond du Lac reservation—a northern Ojibwe reservation. How they ended up in Haḣatoŋwaŋ territory is another story for another day. Jay is a quiet and patient man. He is short, perpetually trim, and light on his feet. His spontaneous and easily contented characteristics are from an earlier drifter lifestyle and later, as a response to coming home. He is quite my opposite—except that I, too, am low to the ground. We are complementary to each other, which I believe is why we have been happily married for so long.

Undoubtedly, Jay has retained the ancestral gene that intuitively signals it is time. He begins the sap harvest by gathering the supplies he keeps stored in one of our boys' abandoned backpacks from their schooldays. He carries the backpack over a

Jay gathers sap from the maples.

shoulder, and with a little hammer his rough brown hands gently tap the metal spigots, called spiles. He puts them in two to three inches through the semi-rough bark into the trunk about three feet up from the ground. Our trees are mature and could handle two spiles, but he only uses one. Then he hangs white food-grade gallon buckets from a small hook connected to the spile to collect the tree sap. The tree sap looks just like ordinary water yet contains approximately 2 percent sugar content. Although he could collect sap until the trees begin budding, he usually stops collect-ing far earlier. Typically, he collects forty gallons each year from the ten maple trees surrounding our front and back yards. As he walks from tree to tree, he pours the sap into five-gallon buckets, covers them, and stores them in the garage until he has enough to begin cooking it down. Weather depending, this will take approx-imately a week to gather as he begins preparing his makeshift wood stove. The outdoor stove is made from an old oil barrel that he sets up in the back of his shed. He will gather cut up wood from our hillside but prefers supplementing from my dad's stash of oak, as it burns hotter than the scrub cedar abundant on our lands. He will start cooking down the sap when he has at least ten gallons ready. The reused roasting basin holds about three gallons that nestles on top of a hole cut in the side of his barrel. Bundled up, he will sit for many hours in his makeshift "sugarbush"—our backyard, composed of a folding chair, a pile of wood, five-gallon pails of tree sap, and the felines circled under his boot-covered feet. While the cooking-down process could be done with consis-tent heat from a propane stove, we prefer the smoky flavor of our maple syrup. Tapping trees and making maple syrup is our first foraging activity as spring awakens.

Wetu, a Dakota word meaning the time of blood, is the time when things grow and renew. It is spring and I can hear the enthu-siasm in the migratory birds flying overhead, returning north once again. I imagine their conversation, "Yes, yes, this is the path we took last year. I can see the all-too-familiar big pond up ahead. Keep flapping. Keep going. We can do it!" Other signs of spring emerge. The grass is greening up and early blooms of bloodroot, western rock jasmine, and the pasqueflower can be found. And we too awaken from our slumber and are ready for renewal.

In the Mni Sota River valley, early spring snowstorms are common and can bring discouragement after being cooped up indoors. Yet, just as these heavy and quick-melting snows leave behind beneficial moisture and nitrogen for emerging perennials and annual crops, we gain enthusiasm and energy for the work ahead. The late Dakota elder Danny Seaboy shared this teaching

Pasqueflower on our lands.

that *wa skaŋ*, those melting snows, are heavy with moisture and leave behind beneficial minerals for the *wato oyate*, the plant nation. The ground is cleansed and the air smells fresh with these final seasonal snowstorms. After the long winter's solitude of reflection and rest, we are ready.

Last year's harvest was plentiful and nourished our family throughout the cold and dark moments and months. We have finished up long-overdue tasks, mended neglected relations and garments. We have told stories of ancestors and place and passed between us the memories of warm summer days. We have shared collected traditions and gifts, recipes, and seeds. We have thoroughly assessed the learnings from last year and reflected on past experiences. We are rested, rejuvenated, and ready to put the new ideas into action. The shifting of seasons is all about change, and while we anticipate this change, the change also changes us. We begin to wake up earlier, we spend more time outside, we may even feel lighter with our sweaters and Netflix put away for warmer days ahead. In *Parable of the Sower*, Octavia Butler poetically writes, "All that you Change / Changes you . . . God / is Change." We are awakened and now ready to set about changes and charter new paths and plans. Let the groundwork and planting begin.

❖   ❖   ❖   ❖

Small-Batch Maple Granola

2 cups oats
$\frac{1}{3}$ cup raw almonds
$\frac{1}{3}$ cup walnuts
1 teaspoon cinnamon
$\frac{1}{2}$ teaspoon salt
$\frac{1}{4}$ cup olive oil
$\frac{1}{4}$ cup maple syrup
$\frac{1}{2}$ teaspoon maple extract
1 cup chopped dried pears, apples

Combine oats, nuts, cinnamon, and salt in a bowl. Mix oil, syrup, and extract. Pour evenly over oats and stir well. Place the mix on a cookie sheet and bake in 350-degree oven for 24 minutes. Stir halfway through. Let mix cool for an hour. Toss granola and chopped dried pears and apples together. Store in an airtight container for up to two weeks.

    I use up my remaining dried pears and apples from the previous season. Using kitchen scissors makes it easier to cut them up into smaller pieces. This granola goes great with a dollop of yogurt for breakfast or just eaten as a snack.

SEEDS OF FAITH

Growing and gardening is a team effort between me and Jay. We have been together for nearly thirty years and can attest to communicating without speech with common thought shared by longtime companions. Years past, we had three additional helpers—our sons, who joined in the seasonal tasks. Today they remain committed to enjoying the fruits of our labor. I anticipate their interest to increase when they start their own families, just as I did. In the early spring, Jay will start preparing the grounds by raking and sometimes burning piles of any remaining spent plants. He will rotate where he makes the burn pile, distributing the residual potash. This natural fertilizer provides potassium, which supports the plants to take in water and in synthesizing sugar for food. He will ask which bed or area I would like prepared first, then next, and so on as I begin planting. He will continue removing weeds and debris and ask if I want a fence or a pile of rotting leaves moved. Over a couple of weeks during this early part of the season, cold-weather plants, including peas, radishes, and spinach, will be sown into the ground. Even a late spring snow-storm will not hurt these crops.

Peas are competitive climbers and so I plant them thick alongside a fence or trellis to support their ambitious climbing. I poke each shriveled green seed in the cold earth about an inch deep. It won't take long before I see the light-green shoots emerging. As they continue to grow, they will send out little tendrils that will curl around the fence wires, making their way up before producing white blossoms, the start of a pod. I prefer to plant the greens and radishes in my raised beds. It makes it easier for me to remove tiny weeds that compete for moisture and nutrients. Once seedlings are up, I will redistribute leftover mulch, such as rotting leaves, grass, and straw, to keep moisture in and weeds out. Planting a row or two every week or so will support continual harvests. I will cease planting greens by early June, having experienced the hot summers in southwest Mni Sota that cause bolting, leading to bitter leaves and roots.

Changing climates have altered our typical planting season. "On or near Good Friday" no longer is our standard timeframe for planting potatoes. The process remains the same, though, starting with cutting the potatoes, ensuring there is an eye on each cut.

My personal goal is to cut the seed potatoes in as many chunks as possible, thus gaining as many plants as possible. However, some years Jay will cut the seed potatoes and I doubt that he holds the same goal, understandably as he is responsible for digging the holes for each cut. After placing a potato piece in each hole, eye up, I will cover them with soil. I will continue to add more soil, mounding up over time, adding more soil as the plants emerge yet keeping the tops exposed to light. The added earth encourages tuber growth from the covered stem, which results in an increased potato harvest. We enjoy eating Yukon Golds and German Butterballs, but also plant a red potato of some kind, perhaps the Pontiac, and a keeper, like a russet. Each provides its distinct flavor and purpose. We have also planted a fingerling in the past and they are tasty fried up, but their crevices are more work to clean. One year, I pressure canned the Yukons, slicing them each in half. They were so delicious fried and cooked up quickly. It reminded me of how my ma canned everything, including chickens. The basement of the old farmhouse from my childhood held rows and rows of canned goods. We never went hungry.

I start the tomato and pepper seeds earlier indoors. Around late March each year, Jay will set up portable shelving with grow lights in the house. Through trial and error, I have learned to start the peppers first as they take longer to grow than tomatoes. In fact, the germination period differs between them as well, with tomatoes germinating in five to ten days and peppers at least two weeks, with hot peppers taking up to four weeks. My timing is better in recent years as I see the pepper plants starting to get blossoms, signaling that I could start hardening them off in about a week. During their time indoors, it is imperative that I keep the light as close to the plants as possible. Otherwise, they stretch, searching for light and making for weak, lanky stems. Once the seedlings emerge into the light, photosynthesis occurs, converting the light into energy whereby the plant's starter leaves will appear. Once they gain their first "true leaves," I transplant the tender seedlings into larger containers. Leftover plastic flowerpots or large plastic cups work just fine. I place a layer of newspaper in the bottom to help keep the moisture from running out of the bottoms. I keep the lights right on top of the plants and slowly raise the lights as they grow. It will look like a jungle by the time I begin weaning the plants. Patience is required during this process. Hardening tomato and pepper plants before planting them in the ground is essential for their survival. They have been nurtured in a climate-controlled environment, and moving them out in the elements of sun, wind, and cool evenings would shock them. So, I use a hardening process that looks like this: day one I move the plants out on the deck late morning for one hour; day two for two hours; day three for three to four hours; and so on. I am careful that for the first few days they are not outside when the temperatures are too hot or too breezy. Because this moving in and out of fifty and up to one hundred plants requires time, I try to time it so that the tomato and pepper plants are both ready for hardening about the same time. Back and forth each day over a week or more, slowly increasing the amount of time each day. Another great trick I learned along the way to support the acclimation process is to turn an oscillating fan on the plants a few weeks before weaning. The air circulation is good for them and the stems toughen up a bit, so they are prepared for the outdoor winds.

SPRING TRADITIONS

Outdoors, while strolling around the yard, I watch for fiddleheads to emerge on the north side of the house and hosta spikes to poke through summer-shaded grounds. Before the unfurling of ferns, the early fiddleheads sautéed in butter and seasoned with salt and pepper make for a tasty dish. Some years ago, we planted asparagus as I was reminded of my grandma Meta. During spring visits to the German side of my extended family, we would drive around looking for asparagus. Grandma Meta was a short lady, a bit chubby with soft skin and caring eyes that took notice of me. She would say, "Keep your eyes peeled," as my brother and I peered out the back car windows in search of asparagus. In hindsight, she must have known where to look because by the time you notice the billowy tops of this perennial that catch your eye when driving side roads the asparagus would be well past their prime. Today, so many of the fields near or in the ditches are sprayed with chemicals, I am not sure I would want to gather asparagus using the same method from my childhood years.

Asparagus officinalis (its scientific name) is part of the lily family and is related to onions and garlic. I recall Jay digging at least six inches down to plant the one-year crowns and fortifying the plantings with some fertilizer. It was three years before we could harvest asparagus spears. But each spring, we can pick it nearly every day by snapping them off at ground level over a period of several weeks. I suspect my childhood memories were my motivation for planting it, but it is a delicious side dish sautéed, baked, or grilled with lemon, garlic, salt, and pepper. I also enjoy sharing it with my dad, imagining it evokes memories for him of "keeping his eyes peeled."

I think, too, of Kuŋśi Genevieve, my Dakota grandma, each spring as I anxiously wait for another perennial crown to emerge. "Rhubarb is a spring tonic, it cleans your blood," she shared many times during springtime visits. It is a delightful memory. Its early harvest of the long red and green stalks cleanses and awakens the sluggish remnants of winter. *Rheum rhabarbarum* is a perennial from the buckwheat family, emerging year after year. Its big leaves are toxic but make for some beautiful art by casting one of the leaves in cement to create a lovely, sculptured garden ornament. But mostly I collect the leaves to suppress the weeds in my beds. When the stalks are long and sufficiently thick, I snap them off at ground level. Jay, just like his mother, eats the rhubarb raw with a bit of salt. It is too tart for my taste. My spring tonic ritual includes rhubarb blended in breakfast smoothies. The spring stimulant renews my blood, heart, and spirit. Likewise, each year a rhubarb crisp or two is in order before the end of harvest. Ma always says you can harvest up until the fourth of July; after that the plant needs to begin storing energy for the following year.

❖   ❖   ❖   ❖

Rhubarb Tonic for Two

4 stalks of rhubarb
2 heaping cups of frozen strawberries
1 banana
6 ounces coconut water
1 tablespoon Chia seeds

Remove leaves from rhubarb—they are poisonous. Clean rhubarb stalks and ends. Chop rhubarb and add to blender along with remaining ingredients. Blend everything until smooth and serve fresh.

A SPIRITUAL EXPERIENCE

Mitakuye makoce kiŋ.

I am sitting on the floor with my legs crossed, my gaze looking out onto *mitakuye makoce kiŋ*, my relative the land. My gaze spans *wato oyate kiŋ*, the plant nation, before I close my eyes. I focus on the light behind my eyes. My sacred essence travels from the base of my skull to the end of my spine. It expands beyond the confines of my dense matter, seeking a grounding space of cosmic comfort and knowing. I imagine my energy, now an illuminating lavender current moving beyond my lighted fingertips and toes, past the greening grasses. It burrows within the cool soils and weaves between entangled roots. An abundance of relatives greets me. Their acceptance is immeasurable. "Hello friends" is all I can whisper, mouth agape, catching tears of elation and immense gratitude. "We are here for you—always," they share without words or whispers but only the sounds a heart can hear. *Mitakuyapi, wopida*, gratitude to my relatives for reminding me that I am connected to all that is.

I benefit from these spiritual experiences of enlightenment at any time through yoga and meditation, from the mat to the gardens, on the deer and rabbit trails through the woods, and during the evening and early-morning stargazing. I feel this same connection through my fingers as I dig them into the cool soils of spring, as they brush across the prairie grasses of summer or touch the orange, magenta, and brown leaves of autumn, or as they gently tap tree branches that release a cascade of winter frost falling and melting across my face as I look up at the blue, blue winter sky.

COMMUNING WITH CREATION

In the spring, as I am planting seeds, my connection and relationship with all of creation is renewed and reminds me there is no separation between me and the seedlings. Faith is planted with each seed and an ongoing cultivation and connection nurtures our symbiotic relationships. To access this *taku wakaŋ* (sacred space and place), I simply walk out my front door. Joy Harjo, Muscogee Creek and our nation's twenty-third poet laureate, shares that in her culture, the new year begins not in the dead of winter on January 1, celebrated with booze, but rather in the spring through honoring plant relatives. In her book *Conflict Resolution for Holy Beings*, Harjo describes the new year when "we become in harmony with each other. Our worlds are utterly interdependent." This makes so much sense to me as spring is about birth and newness.

It is the first of May and birds are singing while I am planting more seeds today. I sense spring is here to stay and fear of any late snows has dissipated. Spinach, kale, flowers, kidney beans, red peanut beans, Dakota popcorn, black turtle beans, white shield beans, and more are faithfully planted. I brought *mni* (water) out with me this time. This is something I usually forgo, typically suffering through a day of planting and then coming in wiped out. It is a layover from the "all or nothing" syndrome I work to recover from. I used to be more concerned about the end goal—to escape the present and live in the future. Practicing mindfulness is no easy feat. So today, I planted and then sat down. I drank some sweet water and rested a bit. Seems simple enough. And yet, I was acutely aware of myself present in this space and the joy that was blossoming in my heart. I took in the sounds of spring and admired the morphosis literally occurring before me. Working now more sustainably, I labored only until noon. I took a seat in one of the handmade Adirondack chairs I competitively won at an auction some years ago. The set of chairs is situated underneath a maple tree that overlooks the garden. On this spring day during the time the Dakota, Mvskoke (Muscogee), and many other Indigenous peoples acknowledge as the New Year, I was rewarded for being in the present. I was greeted by two little sparrows perched on the fence wire singing in harmony.

TEACHINGS AND LESSONS

As I completed my planting tasks, I walked around the garden, making plans for the next plantings. I am also admiring the numerous miracles of seed germination. The peas are looking good and while I admit venison and peas are a tasty combination—I'm praying the *taȟca* (deer) don't find them. The spinach, kale, radish, and onions, too, are poking their heads up through the soil and seeking the light. Do you remember in grade school when we planted a bean seed in a Styrofoam cup and the awe we felt when they sprouted? I relive that childlike feeling each year during the germination stage of planting. We remember from these elementary experiments that all seeds need water, oxygen, and the right temperature, and until those conditions are just right, the seeds remain dormant. When I plant the seed in the ground and water it, the seed takes in water, which scientists call water imbibition. The seed's enzymes and food supplies become hydrated, and the seed coat takes in oxygen, causing the embryo to enlarge. Once it breaks open, a baby root, the radicle, emerges. (The closely related word *radical* is defined as "close to the ground, at the root." We all need to be radical!) Then a plumule emerges, which is the shoot that contains the stem and leaves. The radicle and the plumule are amazingly impressive yet remain fragile as the plant's viability lies in so many subsequent factors. Many things can go wrong during the germination process, which is why I am elated when I see a whole row of sprouts pushing through the soil. When I get radical by lying down on the ground and eyeing closely the new shoots, for example, peas, I can see where the plumule has busted through, sometimes with the outer seed coat still attached. If the ground is too wet, or I water them too much, the seed coat will not open. If I plant the seed too deep, the seed's reserved energy stores will peter out while trying to reach the earth's surface. See what I mean? Our childlike awe was and remains warranted.

We can learn so much by just observing our plant and animal relatives. The Dakota tradition of storytelling, and that of many other Indigenous communities, asserts the importance of learning through observing nature. Mary Louise Defender Wilson, a gifted Dakota storyteller and historian, grew up hearing stories, not just for amusement but as a method of education. She has shared many stories, teaching and passing on lessons—including "The Blue Heron Who Stayed for the Winter," in which values such as hospitality are elevated—or stories that affirm our spiritual connection within the universe, such as "The Star in the Cottonwood Tree." We humans could benefit by returning to childhood practices of story time, coupled with a good nap.

❖   ❖   ❖   ❖

Deer Brats and Noodles

1 pound ziti (or large noodles)
3 venison brats, grilled
½ pint whipping cream
¼ teaspoon cayenne pepper
½ teaspoon garlic powder
6 ounces shredded parmesan cheese
2 cups frozen peas

I like to make this when I have leftover grilled venison brats. While the pasta is cooking, slice the brats into bite-size pieces. Add brats to a large skillet, tossing to lightly char. Add cream and seasonings and stir well. I have used any hot pepper powder that I dry and keep stored in my cupboard. Add most of the parmesan cheese, stirring to melt into the cream. Add the cooked noodles and peas. I will use up last year's frozen garden peas or freshly gathered garden peas. Stir well to coat everything in the creaminess. When everything is heated and incorporated well, serve into dishes and top with remaining cheese. Jay usually gets a scolding for eating up the venison during second helpings, leaving only noodles for the rest of the takers.

SEASONAL CYCLES AND GENERATIONAL PATTERNS

Signs of spring and the coming growing season are everywhere. The raspberries are leafing out, and I search for the garlic I planted last fall. As I move the straw back, their very light green and yellow shoots are poking up. They are searching for light, and I know as soon as I pull the straw away, they will turn the desired shade of green in no time. Other perennials have emerged from their slumber—the rhubarb, hostas, and ferns. Jay is worried that the apple trees will not blossom this year as we had some late frosts. I see the pears are blossoming, though. We have had years with late frosts when the apple trees were affected and produced very little as the freeze killed their delicate buds.

It is Sunday and we are gathering like we used to B.C. (before Covid). The previous year, being on lockdown put a huge damper on our grilling gatherings. But today feels special as we kick off this grilling season with my parents and boys. I decide to acknowledge this memorable moment by holding our picnic outside on the deck. I dress the table with one of the several vintage tablecloths that hold brightly colored flowers and fruit. In addition to the typical variety of *tado* (meat), I made a macaroni-and-pea salad with frozen peas from the year before. It is one of the reasons I decided to plant less this year. It is part of the transition I am working on but finding challenging. My dad has shared that when you get older you just don't eat as much. And while I still eat plenty and am quite "fleshy" (a term my maternal great-grandpa used to describe his mother-in-law), ultimately I have to figure out how to grow and cook for fewer bellies.

After the shared meal, Hepaŋna and I hike the trails after our grilled meal to see if any mushrooms could be found. Tanner, or Hepaŋ (second-born male) as we often call him, is our middle son. While he carries my physical resemblance, except that he towers over me, he carries his dad's demeanor. He is quiet, observant, and very content. He was by far the easiest baby and as a toddler would ask if he could go to bed. "Mama, I tired. Can I go to bed now?" See what I mean—super easy. So, of course a quiet walk observing the landscape would be entertaining for him. We didn't find any mushrooms, but we noticed the lands needed a good rain. I am not into mushrooms but am thrilled by his interest in foraging. I showed him stinging nettle, *caŋicaȟpehu*, which can serve as an edible, a medicinal, and cordage. I have yet to cook up early nettle but have drunk the tea, which is acclaimed for its many benefits. Next, he asked, "What's that?" as he pointed to the many blossoms on nearby bushes. "Those are wild plums. There are several of them," I share, pointing to different areas. *Kaŋta*, wild plums—I can still remember handing my *kuŋśi* a spoonful of wild plum jelly I made after I opened a fresh jar for her on a visit many years ago now. "Oh, gee, that tastes good," I can hear her saying as if it were yesterday, even though she is now long gone from this earthly space. I have imagined that the tart delight elicited her own memories of gathering plums for her *kuŋśi* or preparing her own batch of jam, served on the fresh bread she was renowned for making. I intend to share these memories with Hepaŋna and the other boys, but that day, I held it close. Because of his interest, I eagerly direct him to the gooseberries and other blossoms emerging. I did not take an interest in growing food until I had my first child and so too it might take some time before they have the desire to grow and gather fresh produce. In Carol Schaefer's *Grandmothers Counsel the World*, thirteen Indigenous women elders share that humans need to develop "a deeper, more personal sense of connection with the Earth and our place on it. . . . Seasonal rituals and ceremonies speak to the whole community." My budding hope for this deeper connection is nourished by an image of this same path—yet many springs from now—my Hepaŋna with his hand guiding a future little one who, too, will understand their place on Earth.

✦   ✦   ✦   ✦

Macaroni Pea Salad

1 pound macaroni (elbow or shell)
1½ cups frozen or fresh garden peas
1 small onion, diced
1 tablespoon fresh chopped chives
6 strips cooked bacon, chopped
1½ cup mayonnaise
2 tablespoons white vinegar
1 teaspoon sugar
2 teaspoons crushed dried or chopped fresh parsley
salt/pepper to taste
6 ounces shredded or diced cheddar

Cook pasta al dente; rinse with cold water. Add peas, onion, chives, and chopped bacon. (Chopped ham also works well.) In a small bowl, whisk mayonnaise, vinegar, sugar, and seasonings. Mix into pasta, add cheese, and top with parsley.

CALLS FOR REFLECTION

It is still early May, and I am having a friend over. This is a special occasion in the era of the pandemic. We have gotten our first vaccination shots, and we are both excited to have normal human connections after a year of deprivation. It calls for a special occasion and so I head out to the garden to see what I could harvest for a simple meal. I gathered my first batch of spinach and radish—hooray! I picked some asparagus too.

While gathering, I decide to check on the potatoes to see if they are coming up yet. We planted them over a month ago and I am starting to worry as they do not seem to be sprouting. Potatoes should germinate within two to four weeks. Perhaps it was not warm enough, as they require soil temperatures of 40 degrees. But as I walk down the row of partially covered holes, I begin to count the dark green clusters of thick leaves. "One potato. Two potatoes. Three potatoes! Ah-ah-ah-ah-ah," my head tilted back, as I amuse myself in short Count-like laughs, reminiscent of *Sesame Street* days. I continued to count and find ten potato seedlings are up. Now giddy, I walk over to the kale and this, too, along with the peas is looking good. Everything is coming up, and I reflect again on the magic of germination and the faith we put into the seeds. We poke them into the ground and trustingly hold our breath until they emerge from the soil. And, too, we faithfully wait for the perennials to emerge year after year.

As I continue my slow walk through the garden, licking my cracked lips, I notice how dry the ground is. We need moisture so badly in what should be the rainy period. How will this summer be if we are starting out the season already water deficient? I think back on other years. Yes, this definitely should be the rainy season. Holding memories of Hepaŋna's graduation party a few years back, I recall a friend and I had walked the trails. We were astounded by numerous orange jelly-like globs hanging from the cedar trees. After some research, I had learned it was a fungus that emerges during wet years. Thinking back on another spring, the east hillside was filled with pasqueflowers right near our "zen space." This year, I found one lonely, pitiful one. Today, I walk down to our zen space, sit on the cedar bench Jay made for me, and rest my feet on a downed cedar log. Jay and my dad had cleared this spot so that I could watch and listen to the flow of Boiling Springs Creek below. It is a hillside space worthy of solitude, reflection, and gratitude. What is my responsibility to this creek and the lands that hold the precious water we rely upon?

I think about water more than ever during these seemingly unprecedent times of drought. *Mni wiconi*—"water is life"—is now an often-quoted phrase across Turtle Island. During 2016–17, many people across the world joined in solidarity with the Standing Rock Sioux Tribe to fight against the multi-billion-dollar oil pipeline to protect sacred sites and fresh water. Water protectors joined in prayer, ceremony, marches, and demonstrations along the Missouri and Cannonball Rivers in North Dakota. The pipeline runs underneath Lake Oahe, the tribe's source of water. I don't need to wonder how I would feel if a corporation chose to run a pipe of oil near the abundant aquifer we rely upon. I think upon the generations of Dakota people who gathered near this creek, undoubtedly an abundant source of freshwater as it runs year-round. One of the first years after we moved here, the neighbors took me and Gaby, a close friend and relative to Jay, and our kids, down to the source of the spring. The spot where the water bubbles up and joins the creek lies on their land. While vegetation covered much of the area, a pool of fresh water marked this spot. As we adults took in the historical, cultural, and spiritual importance of this site, my two youngest jumped straight into the pool of cool waters. My neighbor laughed at their spontaneity and their apparent lack of concern for the muck and leeches, no beach, and perhaps the clear lack of approach. My two little chubby brown otters splashing around reminded me, too, of the joy that this body of water had provided to our people long ago.

Mni wiconi certainly isn't a new phrase. Our people have known that water is life, water is alive, and we are utterly dependent upon clean water. I can even draw on the words "*Mni wiconi kiŋ he yukaŋ; Ota ota ota.*" These are words found in the song "The Water of Life" in the *Dakota Odowaŋ* (Dakota book of songs). And while the translated words, "The water of life is to be for many," imply baptism, I can conclude that the life-giving water that flows in my back yard and yours is to be for all of us, not just for those living now but for those future seven generations.

✦　　✦　　✦　　✦

Simple Roasted Asparagus

asparagus
olive oil
seasoning
lemon

Set your oven to 350 degrees. Clean asparagus stalks. With a vegetable peeler, strip a bit of the thicker, tough outside layer on the

recipe continued ▶

lower end of the stalks. Although this step is not necessary,
it removes any stringiness and ensures more tender bites. Place
the stalks in a bowl and drizzle with olive oil, salt, and pepper
and toss together. You can also add minced garlic if desired. Place
the seasoned and oiled stalks on a cookie sheet (or I like to use
stoneware). Bake for 8–10 minutes. It also works fine to sauté or
throw them on the grill in tinfoil. Squeeze a fresh lemon over the
stalks and serve immediately. This dish pairs well with a juicy
steak and baked potato.

AN ACT OF FAITH

I am admiring them—the nicest-looking peppers I have ever
seeded. I have been weaning them, moving them back and forth
from outside and back inside for the past week. I imagine how the
real sunshine feels good to their leaves, stems, down to their soul
roots, rather than the faux light buzzing above them that nourished them to life. In and out, just like my boys during their childhood days, getting ready for adulthood. The seedlings received a
treat during one of their acclimation periods, a little rain shower.
The near-adult peppers and me on the front deck and their surrounding relatives all opened up in a chorus of joy, breaking the
dusty spring drought. It was going to be all right.

That was until Rasta the brute. Rasta, sometimes called Pasta,
is an eighty-pound Rottweiler Lab, mixed with some Australian
shepherd. Her then nearly two-year-old body and mind were
pouting. She felt neglected as we were immersed in work over
a series of days, prepping our gardens, doting on seedlings, in
between Zoom calls. I stepped out to the porch for a breath of
spring air, a reprieve from the computer screen. To my horror,
I witnessed fragments of at least three peppers strewn around
the yard outside of their nourishing soil-and-plastic-container
homes. I hadn't heard their silent screams during the carnage.
One was completely executed, beheaded, its stark stem sticking
out and void of any leaves. It would be unable to be revived. Oh,
the sight of it was awful. I picked up what I could, including the

deceased one, stuffing the mangled pepper plant on top of its dead relative, hoping and willing it to survive.

I take a few minutes to scold the murderer. "Bad dog! *Iya-ya!* Get out of here! I can't believe you did this! Go!" I gather the remaining intact relatives and bring them indoors, saving them from any more potential injury. I give the survivors lifesaving water, including one that appears unconscious, completely drooped over. The other, literally shaking. I stop just to observe her. I coo over her a bit. I tell her, "It will be okay." Slowly, she settles, and her shaking subsides.

Later that evening, I tenderly check on them again. Soothing myself, I say aloud, "All living things have a strong desire to live." Later, I rely on this thought to lull me to sleep. But as soon as I awaken, I check on my beloveds. I am overjoyed because I am now sure of it. Their tender stems have pulled themselves back upright and their small leaves are fluffed back up a bit. All living things *do* have a desire to live. They will live and I assure them that they will be planted today in their new home, safe from the brute.

✦   ✦   ✦   ✦

Stuffed Peppers

4 large, whole bell peppers, all seeds and membranes removed
1 pound buffalo burger
1 onion, chopped
2 cloves garlic, finely chopped
2 cups cooked rice (white, brown, or wild rice works fine)
1 jar homemade salsa
salt and pepper
4 ounces shredded cheddar cheese

Cook buffalo burger and add onion when meat is cooked halfway through. When nearly done, add garlic. In a large bowl add cooked burger, cooked rice, salsa, salt, and pepper. Scoop the mix into peppers (there will likely be remaining burger and rice mix that you can use in a hotdish). I use tinfoil to help prop up peppers and gently cover them. Bake in oven at 350 degrees for 45 minutes. Remove tinfoil, top with cheese, and bake for another 15 minutes.

A SONG AND A DANCE

We had a frost advisory last night. It is still cool for late May, but I have decided to go out and check on a few things in the garden. As I round the corner of the house I stop in my tracks. Oh, it is one of the most beautiful sounds! I walk past the pear trees toward the apple trees and am completely enamored—their limbs are loaded with blush-colored blossoms. I stand under the tree and look up to fully take in the beauty of the song and dance the bees are making. I am raptured as my ears take in the hum of their wingbeat song seemingly in unison. My eyes attempt to follow the pollinators, which is completely impossible as they dance from blossom to blossom. My heart is filled as I think about the nectar and pollen they are collecting and taking back to their home. The bees will stick with one plant at a time, in this case the apple blossom, going back and forth until there is nothing more to gather. Perhaps that is why there are so many at one time at the apple tree today. The abundance of apple blossoms will have them coming back for more over the short stint of a few days. I imagine they are overjoyed by the abundance of food, as I am thrilled by the number of apples their work will produce.

According to the Pollinator Partnership's "About Pollinators" page, we have pollinators to thank for every one out of three bites of food. Can that really be true? I ask myself. I decide to check. Are the bees responsible for my morning coffee? Through a quick search I learn that coffee bean plants are self-pollinating, a process whereby pollen transfers to the stigma from the same plant or blossom to blossom from the same plant. But hold on! Bees still help with pollination of the coffee beans and in some cases are responsible for up to 50 percent of the beans produced. Plus, they improve the quality and size of the bean. With this information I decided yes, I have the bees to thank for coffee because the coffee we drink is delicious and abundant. But what about the cream and sugar I add? Cream, obviously not—thank you, cows, but then I think, what do cows eat? Grasses and corn. I know from growing corn that it is pollinated through the wind and that corn is a developed form of grass. So, I can safely say no. What about sugar? I scanned the internet and learned that sugar canes are asexual and do not require pollinators. Their stems have a node that when planted produces primary roots, similar to potatoes or even the numerous succulents that Caske (my oldest son, Hunter) has prop-agated using this process. What about my breakfast? I had yogurt, swirled with maple syrup, and pineapple. Yogurt falls in the cream category, so that is a no. Maple syrup was harvested from the maple trees. I learn that maple trees are pollination generalists, which means that pollination methods vary, involving the wind and bees, as well as self-pollination. Okay, well, our maple syrup comes from our very own Autumn Blaze maple trees. This search proves more challenging. I then learn that they are a hybrid between red maples and silver maples, and they are known as fast-growing trees. But they can be top heavy and structurally weak, making them prone to wind damage. Without going any further down the rabbit hole, I mark this as a maybe or a both/and. How about pineapples? Oh wow! Hummingbirds and bats pollinate this delicious fruit. While I knew that bees, birds, butterflies, and wasps were all respon-sible for transporting pollen from one blossom to another, I had no idea that small mammals like bats and lemurs also help with pollination. I think of bats getting stuck in your hair and eating mosquitoes but had no idea that they pollinate more than five hundred plants worldwide. We need bats too! On to lunch, which was a turkey sandwich with greens on wheat bread, pickles, and a glass of tea. I can already guess that the tea plant is a yes and a quick search confirms that bees pollinate it, the *Camellia sinensis*. We already learned that grains are a no. Obviously turkey is a no, but what about the lettuces and arugula that I topped my sand-wich with? These I learn are self-pollinating, but cross-pollination can occur with bees, and I make a mental note of this for future seed-saving among my greens. I already know that the cucumbers turned pickles are a yes because I have often watched bees move from one yellow blossom to the other in my dad's annual cucum-ber patch. But what about the glass of wine I enjoy at the end of the day? No, grapevines have both male and female parts and thus are self-pollinating. However, I stumbled across an article that discusses the soil needs of grapevines that require diverse cover crops such as mustard and clover, which do require bees. I am starting to get the feel of this research. It seems as though in every meal there is a solid yes, followed by a no, but that leads to an indirect connection through complementary plants for improved soils or increased production. I decide not to complete the research on a potato soup supper, knowing that the other vegetables in the pot are likely a yes with the potatoes a no, but that the meat and dairy products are a, well, maybe. While I wish I could say I will carry this lesson with me at each meal, I know that I am a forgetful human being who often takes for granted the work of our pollinators. But for this evening, I am full of gratitude for the song and dance of our bee relatives. *Tuḣmaġa oyate kiŋ wopida uŋkenciyapi ye!* (We say thanks to you the bee nation!)

❖   ❖   ❖   ❖

Potato Soup

2 stalks celery
1 large onion
2 tablespoons butter
3 cloves garlic
1 quart chicken/vegetable broth
3–4 potatoes (Yukons are delish!)
1–2 teaspoons salt
1–2 teaspoons white pepper
2 tablespoons fresh chopped chives
2–3 cups water
4–6 strips cooked bacon, chopped
$\frac{1}{2}$–1 cup heavy cream or half & half

Clean and chop celery and onion. Heat soup pot on medium heat and add butter. When hot, add celery and onion. Mince the garlic and add. Stir and add the broth. Clean and dice potatoes and add. Season with white pepper, salt, and chives. Add enough water to cover and cook potatoes, considering desired consistency of soup—less for thick, creamy soup or more for broth texture. When potatoes are nearly done, add bacon. (Diced ham works as well.) Before serving, add heavy cream, stir to heat.

INTERDEPENDENCY

After a meal of grilled burgers and fresh asparagus, Jay took off to go fishing at a local marsh. Tyson Lake is so small only the locals know of it. I wonder if anyone thinks of Joseph Tyson, the local pioneer and homesteader it is named for. Not me. I think of our Dakota people who were displaced from these lands. My ancestors would have known all the local fishing spots, Bde Caŋ and Hiŋta Haŋkpa Woźu, for example. Both these lakes are in the same vicinity of Tyson Lake. *Bde Caŋ*, or Wood Lake, is now part of Timm Park, a popular county campground likely named in honor of another white guy. According to Paul Durand's *Atlas of the Eastern Sioux* and Warren Upham's *Minnesota Place Names: A Geographical Encyclopedia*, Hiŋta Haŋkpa Woźu is just two miles west of Bde Caŋ. Durand and Upham describe the lake, now extinct, as the Dakota planting gardens of the Basswood Moccasin Thong Band. They share a story of how the particular Waȟpetoŋwaŋ Band (Dwellers among the leaves) acquired the name as told by Louis Garcia, an honorary tribal historian of, and who married into, the Spirit Lake Nation. Why change all the names of these places? The renaming of lakes and more feels like an intentional erasure of the original people of these lands. Further, what I believe is truly lost in the renaming is that names like Tyson and Timm do not remind me of my connection and relationship to place. But learning the meaning and story behind Hiŋta Haŋkpa Woźu draws me in. The history and culture of a place remind me of the interdependence between me and the waters, lands, plants, and animals.

The same deep connection and interdependence are gained when we find "cultural artifacts" on our lands. Each spring, as the ground heaves and thaws, we find rocks that were obviously shaped and utilized as tools. Fitting perfectly in our hands, they could serve to grind, crush, rub, chop, cut, and perhaps even hold dyes. As the rocks rest in my hands, I sense the ancient hands that once held them and wonder about their daily lives. Crawling around in the wooded hillside, amongst scraggly cedars and before the grass comes up, I search for golf balls from Jay's practice swings. During one particular venture among overgrown bushes, I found two fire pits made of rocks. While the pits were no longer perfectly circular and the rocks were now partially covered by earth and moss, it's still easy to imagine people gathered around the fires they held. Jay shares that these "finds" provide him with a sense of belonging to this place—a township where we are the only Dakota inhabitants. What's more, I reflect on our care of this land and what kind of historical and cultural evidence we will leave behind generations from now—will it be one that reflects care of land, water, future generations, and our interconnectedness?

While Jay was on his quest for some walleye, I stayed back because I hadn't picked up a fishing license yet, and so decided to make honey oat buns and cookies for tomorrow's family dinner. I am quite sure he just wanted to try out the fat worms he had been collecting for bait from the garden as he cleaned up and prepared beds for my planting. He would drop his line in the water just off the dock. He exercised catch and release on several bullheads. But eventually Jay did bring in the fish he was looking for.

As he was on his way home, I noticed the fading light while I finished up baking. I muttered to myself about who was going to be cleaning fish this late in the day. Just then, he walked in beaming with a decent sized walleye on his stringer. I didn't wait for the answer when I asked who was going to be cleaning the fish. I got up from the recliner in my pajamas and told him to get me some newspaper and to sharpen the fillet knife. Rasta joined me on the deck, sniffing and licking her lips. Would I remember how to fillet fish the way dad had taught me? It took a bit longer than the week's end of last year's fishing trip, but it did all come back to me. I managed not to puncture the lungs, anus, or guts, carving out two nice fillets. I washed them and put them in a freezer bag. Tomorrow I am heading to town for my fishing license.

RESTORATION

I sat on the ground in the garden planting multiple crates of prairie sage. With each hole I dug, I would uncover a rock or two. The back part of our garden has always been a challenging area. I have tried planting crops over the years only to be a bit disappointed. This area has a lot of clay and what we call crabgrass. While we have attempted to add tilth to this area through leaves, grass clippings, compost, and peat moss, it just never seemed quite enough. So, a few years ago I decided to plant perennials that I thought might survive or even do well in this type of soil. First, I planted three aronia berry bushes. I chose aronia because a friend had baked them in lieu of blueberries in a sweet bread she shared. Having always wanted to grow blueberries but hearing how difficult they are to cultivate without the ideal acidic soil conditions, I decided on aronias. *Aronia melanocarpa*, commonly called chokeberries, do prefer slightly acidic soils but are less finicky. Well, mine did not do well right away until I added some organic fertilizer and watered them more regularly. Last year I gathered a few handfuls of berries from two of the three bushes. But this year, they are loaded with blossoms. As I read up on them, sources recommend added nutrients and consistent watering at first and after a few years the plant becomes more adapted to its environment. Huh, how ironic! I am relieved to read this after investing three to four years in them, knowing this perennial was a good selection for this area.

The next plants I added a few years ago were three types of *ceyaka* (mint)—apple mint, spearmint, and peppermint. As I've learned from others, *ceyaka* is prolific and spreads like crazy. It did not take long for my varieties to take off. One of the fun things to do during a garden tour is to have people try each of the mints for a breath freshener. I also love to see their faces when I hand them a cup of cold mint tea. How refreshing!

Then there is the rhubarb I had originally planted on the other side of the yard. It has never done well. It always starts out great but then when the trees are fully leafed out, it is a bit too shady for the plant to produce more than one small cutting. Or at least that is why I think they don't prosper. So, during the fall a few years ago, we dug up chunks of each plant and transplanted them in this back garden area. This is the second spring they have emerged. Last year we had a drought, so I cannot speculate on the pending success. This year they are up and growing but still are not robust enough to harvest. I will wait one more year to decide if I should redig them and move them to a different area.

We have also tried a few random plantings in this area. Once I planted a whole row of tobacco. I was thrilled because it all came up from the teeny tiny seeds. Unfortunately, I failed to alert Jay that the seedlings were in fact intentional, and he hoed them up to their demise. Two years ago, I planted ground cherries I had diligently seeded in the house weeks and weeks earlier. They did fantastic! But I was the only one interested in unwrapping the sweet yellow globes. I had hoped they would carry on reseeding themselves, but it did not come to fruition, which was fine because late last summer, as I walked along the edge of prairie grasses near the road, I found what looked like similar plants. They had the same little papery lanterns close to the ground. I tried eating one only to disappointedly spit it out. This year, I am trying to grow a few seedlings in a pot. They are taking a long time to grow robust, but I still have hope. Some friends gave us a grape vine that we planted two years ago in the same area. It is still alive, and we are hopeful to witness its maturity. That same year, I dropped a packet of perennial flower seeds near the stubby grape vine. But I cannot seem to remember the name of them. They grow very tall and have beautiful combs of periwinkle blossoms. I will have to do some research once it flowers again to reidentify the hearty perennial as it does quite well in this area of prairie soil.

Finally, this brings me to the seventy-plus holes I dug for the prairie sage in this same area. Our tribe's Office of the Environment provided crates of this indigenous plant to any of our tribal citizens who wanted them. I have a small batch of a different variety of sage growing on the side of the house, mostly under the eaves. It gets random waterings when we remember and from

side driving rains from the west but mostly it is a dry area. I suspect that the sage I planted over the last two evenings is going to
be happy and abundant in these resistant original soils.

✦   ✦   ✦   ✦

Ceyaka Waḣpe

Gather a good bunch of mint. Rinse and shake to get rid of
remaining bugs or spiders, or gently rinse with water. Fill a four-
quart pot with water. Bring the water to a simmer, then shut off.
Add the mint and cover the pot. Steep for 20 minutes or until
water cools. Strain mint from the water and refrigerate steeped
water or enjoy immediately. Serve hot or cold with ice.

   I also dry the varieties of mints throughout the season,
preferably before they flower so that they can go to seed. I also
think the mint tastes too strong or a little bitter to use late in the
season. I use dried mint for hot tea throughout the year and also
add a few teaspoons to a green smoothie for a refreshing bang.

TRUTH TELLING AND ACKNOWLEDGMENT

It is early June, not quite summer with the solstice still two weeks
away. Yet the grass is a lush green, the trees are in full bloom, and
the *capoŋka* (mosquitoes) are already out. I slap another one
trying to suck the blood out of my tanned fleshy arm, wondering how we will get through an interview shoot without their
distractions. Dekśi and I are meeting with a film crew who have
come from the National Native American Boarding School Healing Coalition in Bloomington, Minnesota, a city 113 miles east of
us. They are interviewing survivors and descendants of boarding
school victims. My grandparents Genevieve and Walter LaBatte Sr.
attended Indian boarding schools.

   My *kuŋśi*, at a mere six years old, along with her sisters went
to the Pipestone Indian Boarding School. I shared the little bit
that I know of her experience as she did not talk much about it.
Only after I questioned my grandmother about her time at boarding school and what she learned, did she share that she liked it

because she learned how to cook and sew. It was not the response I had expected to hear, having read and heard of the many horrific experiences others had. After researching and learning more of our family's history I came to understand her life. She was motherless at the age of two—her mother died, leaving all five girls with their father. Perhaps she appreciated learning what should have been typical knowledge and skills gained through a mother–daughter relationship. She did recognize that she was quite young to be away from home. She said, "I was so young I had to stay with the matrons." In my opinion, no matter the age, it just should not have been. The whole boarding school policy was a generational disaster, leaving the children traumatized from physical, spiritual, mental, and sexual abuse. I do not know if my grandmother experienced any of these traumas, but I cannot imagine the heartache felt from being lonesome for all the comforts of family and home.

Closer to her passing, she shared that perhaps she and her sisters may have been treated better "on account of my father." I wish I had asked more about what she meant because I do not know if it was because her father, my great-grandfather, Waŋbdiska (White Eagle), was a white man or if it was because of his stature or both. Fred Pearsall, my great-grandfather, was an educated man who spoke several languages, including Dakota, and for all purposes, lived as a Dakota. As a result of his life experiences and acceptance of both societies, he served as a translator for the government. My uncle shares that Fred Pearsall often translated for probate issues, helping officials understand the line of kinship among the parties, whether blood or *huŋka* (adopted, taken as a relative in the Dakota tradition). Uncles being fathers, aunties being mothers, cousins being siblings, and numerous grandparents, as was and remains the tradition of Dakota people. Making relatives of nearly everyone is a strength of Dakota culture, weaving relationships and all the benefits and responsibilities that go with being in relationship. Yet, this can make for difficult decisions regarding heirship of land. Of course, this too should not have been, because Mni Sota Makoce ought to belong to all of the Dakota Nation.

I wrap up the boarding school conversation to emphasize that truth telling is necessary for healing to occur. We have a lot of dysfunction in our families and communities as a result of boarding schools, such as corporal punishment for disciplining children. This is not how we originally raised our children. To change things and to heal, we must acknowledge and understand the origins—colonization.

Finishing up the interview, I see Dekši approaching. Uncle has on his typical attire—a pair of blue jeans, a western shirt, and his cowboy hat. I smile and comment, "Hey, Dekši, we're matching," as we both have on a bright pink-colored shirt. I tell the camera man to interview him, too, as he is one step closer and will have more to share. Dekši rolls with the impromptu interview, and I get up from the bench and decide I need to take a walk to shake off the conversation. Uncle and I are here for a storytelling event at the Gideon Pond House to share our new book, *Voices from Pejuhutazizi: Dakota Stories and Storytellers.* I had only arranged this interview location for convenience. I walk around the yard of the park that is now owned by the city of Bloomington. I take in all that is lush and green, including the view overlooking the hillside. It is breathtaking and I almost forget that we are in the city. That is until I hear the planes fly overhead. Strolling to clear my mind, I walk over to the shell of an *inipi* lodge (used for sweat/purification ceremonies) nestled up to vegetative overgrowth. Someone has planted strawberries and a three sisters garden of beans, corn, and squash. One of the board members of the historic site walks over to me and asks if we are ready, and I join him and others who have come to hear story.

It doesn't go unnoticed by me that Uncle, Jay, and I are the only Dakotas in the room. Through conversation we uncover that descendants of Gideon Pond, Thomas Williamson, and Joseph Renville are in the audience. Pond and Williamson were early missionaries living among Dakotas in this location and prior, at Cloud Man's Village in what became Minneapolis on the eastern side of Bde Maka Ska (White Earth Lake), later renamed Lake Calhoun, and now renamed Bde Maka Ska again. Gratitude to sisters

Kate Beane and Carly Bad Heart Bull for their heroic efforts in reclaiming the Dakota place name. Joseph Renville, who was both Dakota and Canadian French, helped Williamson and Pond with creating a Dakota alphabet and orthography—a writing system to learn and teach Dakota, with the intention to Christianize the people. The storytelling tendency of my uncle brings out a family story, one that I had not heard. He recounts how we are related to Joseph Renville, who is the brother of Ohiya (Victor) whose son was Tiwakaŋ (Sacred Lodge), also known as Gabriel Renville. Joseph in part raised Tiwakaŋ because his own father, Ohiya, had died. Often missionaries demanded that Dakota completely abandon their traditional ways in order to take on the Christian religion. Dekši tells that Tiwakaŋ held on to and practiced Dakota traditions, including having three wives. Having more than one wife has less to do with what people assume and more to do with care and responsibility to extended family. This practice was unacceptable to missionary Stephen Riggs. Uncle tells us, though, that Thomas Williamson, whose great-great-grandson is in the audience, had a different opinion. Thus, Tiwakaŋ was able to become a Presbyterian while retaining his Dakota traditions.

Dekši and I round out our talk taking turns telling stories—he shared his memories and I read from our book. I am counting on repeatedly hearing his stories during our book tour so that I can absorb and be able to recount these stories long after he is gone. I recognize that storytelling is his gift and mine is writing. We pack up afterward and once again I am grateful for my partner, who quietly waits in the wings, hauls items back to the car, and drives us home.

We share stories on the way of boarding school reflections and talk about how it impacted our own parenting and observations and conversations we had with the afternoon's participants. He tells about the discussion he had with the caretaker of the historic site, who is the great-great-great-grandson of the missionary Pond. He holds out his hand, revealing two dwarf ears of corn. The kernels are made up of two colors—matte blue and off-white. One cob is white and the other the rust red that I have on rare occasion seen in my own Indian corn. It is a sign of cross-pollination with field corn. Jay recounts all that was shared with him. The site's caretaker and ancestor to Pond was gifted some of the corn that came from a cave in Utah. That corn was estimated to be more than three hundred years old. The caretaker planted his gifted ancient kernels, and they grew! He has been trying to maintain the corn with last year's and this year's crop each producing only one stalk. I recognize the challenge and opportunity to grow this corn out. It will take years to create viability with the handful of kernels coming from two mere cobs and one being tainted. I think, too, with truth telling—it'll take years to flush out the tainted that has taken up space. When I reflect on the generations that have gone through our education systems, void of Indigenous knowledge, voices, and contributions, and the whitewashing of history, including the theft of land that this country was founded on— I recognize it is going to take a lot of effort and time for us to grow learners and leaders with robust and foundational understandings. Speaking with honesty, acknowledging our collective past, and healing will take years, perhaps beyond my lifetime.

❖   ❖   ❖   ❖

Three Sister Salad

2 cups of cooked wild rice
2 cobs sweet corn, cooked, kernels cut from cob
1½ cups cooked black beans
1 medium zucchini, diced
¼ cup chopped jalapeños
1 medium red onion, diced

Dressing
½ cup chopped cilantro
½ cup extra-virgin olive oil
3 tablespoons fresh lime juice
2 tablespoons water
1 tablespoon apple cider vinegar
2 teaspoons honey
1 teaspoon garlic salt
½ teaspoon dried oregano
pepper to taste

recipe continued ▶

Toss together the rice, corn, beans, zucchini, jalapeños, and red onion. Sweet corn can be swapped with *wamnaheza (corn)*, once it has been lyed and cooked. Whisk the remaining ingredients in a separate bowl to make a vinaigrette. Combine with other ingredients. Let sit in refrigerator for at least a few hours for flavors to combine.

PROCLAMATION

It is dusk, around nine o'clock on a Sunday evening. I am tired after a long week of work and travel, and I decide to step out on the back porch. Bees and other insects are busily taking in the fresh scene of abundant nectar. It is incredible to be up this close to them as they shove their whole head into one of the many blooms. They are there for a couple of seconds before they plop into another nearby bloom. I stop to observe one of the bees—a fat, furry bumblebee. This time the angle provides me a close look at their black pointy tongue, which I later learn is called the maxillae, a sheath for its feathery tongue. I slowly begin to bring my head nearer to the cluster of blooms when the bee flaps its wings to rise and buzzes right past my face. I take this as a sign to buzz off and sigh. Later, I research Minnesota bumblebees and learn there are twenty-four of them. The rusty-patched bumblebee is our state bee. Yet, the U.S. Fish and Wildlife Service assessed and listed the rusty-patched bumblebee on the endangered list in 2017. While the data are not definitive, several combined factors may be the cause for their decline, including pesticides, habitat loss, and the effects of climate change. I make a mental note to take photographs in an attempt to document which bumblebee species are enjoying the wisteria's periwinkle clusters of sweet-scented blossoms.

The wisterias we planted several years ago have done exactly what we hoped for. All of the three vines made their way up the cedar posts, albeit with a little coaxing. After that, they ambitiously twisted and turned all on their own, braiding their way to the deck and rails and finally up the lattice Jay added. This he did to create an enclave to hang a hammock for me. It provided a

Bumblebee on wisteria on back deck.

tiny oasis to relax in. I am gently swinging, and the buzzing is all around me when I hear a single bird's voice. It doesn't seem to be a song but more of a proclamation. The bird's voice is quite loud. It sounds as if we are in an outdoor amphitheater, and it occurs to me that the surrounding leafed-out trees are in a way holding sound in this space. It is quite incredible to hear this bird, and I so wish I knew our local birdsongs and voices beyond the distinguishable crows, blue jays, robins, and red-winged blackbirds.

What could this storytelling bird be sharing? "Relatives: Today was another beautiful day. Be grateful for the abundance we have. Let us give our gratitude to the worms and insects for giving up their lives so that we may live. Let us also give thanks to the trees and bushes for they have provided safety and a home. Our gratitude for the creek below us that quenches our thirst and the pools of water to bathe in. And let us not forget brother snake and sister squirrel. For they, too, were chosen by Creator to live in this paradise. May we all awaken to rejoice and express our gratitude once again when Mother Earth turns toward the light. *Wopida, wopida, wopida.*" Then all is quiet except for the distant croak of an American toad and the rhythmic chirping of crickets. It seems as if our feathered friends did, in fact, go to sleep, and I am beyond grateful to have been able to take in this sweet evening edict.

Bdoketu

THE SACRED CACHE

Cool clumps break apart in my hands
fulfilling my longing to touch the earth.
An awaited desire released,
Freeing mist as she stirs.

Last year's chosen
greeted by her.
Hand, palm, and from secret caches they come
stretching across spells and spans of time.
Entrusted to her
sprinkled with conviction from family and kin,
they swell and ascent, reaching towards infinite blue sky
their succession nourishing ours
from generations past,
celebrated gifts of omnipresence,
and an inheritance to the willing.

Summer
The Time of the Potato

TO REMEMBER

Summertime in Indian country is abundant in ceremony, in the making and renewing of relatives, and of honoring and celebrations. In the garden, so, too, I am immersed in seasonal rituals, carrying traditions into the garden, on lands, in the woods, and near water. I tend to plant relatives—we weed and hoe, water and feed, nurture and care for them in hopes of harvesting an abundance come fall. Celebrations and honoring, which is an act of remembrance, occurs each time we offer gratitude, our prayers, and in the sharing and gifting to others. These acknowledge the abundance our plant relatives provide, their sustenance, medicine, teachings, and connection. In *Braiding Sweetgrass*, Indigenous scientist Robin Wall Kimmerer shares an exquisite treasure of plant knowledge that affirms the seasonal teachings and gifts I experience in my garden, the woods, the waters, and land that I return to over and over for encouragement and wisdom. Kimmerer writes, "Ceremonies are the way we remember to remember." The garden offers a sanctuary for remembrances, reflections, and ponderings. As I stroll along the pathways between plants and garden beds, I ask myself, "What am I remembering to remember today?" What am I recalling and reclaiming through these repeated sacred exchanges between *Ina Maka* (Mother Earth), *wato oyate kiŋ* (the plant nation), and *miye* (me)?

Today, through the recesses of my mind, I draw upon a remembered science lesson from grade school—the water cycle. Water evaporating, condensation building, and then eventually coming down as precipitation. I realize that is far too simplistic for the many factors that contribute to the cycle of water. But the takeaway for me is the same. The water is cycled over and over again. Despite the earth being covered in 70 percent water, most of it is in the oceans and less than 1 percent of it is actually fresh, drinkable water for all living things. It is divided between lakes (.26 percent), atmosphere (.04 percent), wetlands (.03 percent), and rivers (.006 percent). Right now, during these long stretches without needed moisture, I remember to take a deep breath of gratitude when that cycle returns again as rain. This year's drought in Mni Sota Makoce (Land of Cloudy Waters, more commonly phrased as "Land of 10,000 Lakes") causes me to gain a deeper understanding and appreciation that truly *water is life.* It was so dry this year that I had even wondered if the aquifer that feeds our well would go dry. We had been told by the previous owners that our well would *never* go dry. Yet, I heard reports of spigots drying up in rural areas of our state during this climactic year. Too, a neighbor shared that their water levels dropped so low they had to wait days for it to replenish before they could shower. Where did the water go? Are we contributing to the disruption of the water cycle?

As I scan the Global Precipitation Measurement maps on the National Aeronautics and Space Administration (NASA) website, it's clear that precipitation is interrelated all around the earth. Something somewhere has obviously caused changes in our area. We hear reports of people finding skeletons and ancient ships once buried beneath water in two of our big rivers—the Minnesota and Mississippi Rivers. Will river water data decrease from the mere .006 percent of our planet's fresh water? And if so, where does the water go? Perhaps it has become a part of the atmospheric moisture that has been dumping huge amounts of hurricane storms in the southeast or the flooding that European countries have experienced lately. What other ways are we perhaps taking this precious gift for granted?

According to the Environmental Protection Agency, in the United States the largest use of freshwater is for thermoelectric power (think coal, oil, gas, nuclear) and irrigation (think agriculture), which together account for 77 percent. Additionally, the Geological Survey (USGS), which conducts a report of our nation's and state's water use every five years, reports that cities and towns use 11 percent and 1 percent for domestic purposes of Earth's freshwater, respectively. I guess I shouldn't be surprised by these stats, but I am. However, I am encouraged by the increased efforts in clean energy practices that benefit the environment by sustaining freshwater sources. For example, a local coal-burning energy plant retired more than a decade ago was recently torn down, and rural solar farms are seemingly popping up everywhere. At the same time, agriculture in our area seems to be expanding, stripping groves and tree lines to bring in more money. This aligns with one of the USGS reports I read that indicated a trend in lower water use to generate thermoelectric power while at the same time water use for irrigation is increasing. I am not suggesting we stop power production or large-scale farming—I value electricity and love my bowl of oatmeal as much as the next person. Still, I wonder if our technology and drive for producing more need to evolve by factoring in the impact on water and other finite resources.

There's a local hotspot, a winery a mile down the road. It is a beautiful and picturesque scene of giant cottonwoods, the creek, and the vineyard. We often take friends and family there to enjoy a glass of vino and the best-tasting pizza around. This little treasure in the southwestern part of our state doesn't seem like a threat to our water cycle. Yet sipping my glass of wine got me thinking about the national discussion regarding California wine production taking up too much precious water. The incessant drought patterns, fires, and water wars in the west have me wondering just how much water it takes to make the glass of wine I so enjoy. Through a little online searching, I find that the answer varies. Reports range anywhere from two to six gallons for a gallon of wine. That is without adding in irrigation numbers. Water is not just used in the irrigation of vineyards, but a significant amount is used in cleaning the equipment needed to produce the wine. With it factored in, the numbers are wildly high and vary greatly, but one estimate reported in a 2015 article, "Water to Wine," that appeared on the website of the Yale Center for Business and the Environment, is twenty-nine gallons for one five-ounce glass of wine. Gulp! My heart sinks as I contemplate forgoing my oft evening treat. I read some more, and my guilt begins to dissipate. Research and development are underway to reduce water usage, through, for example, drip irrigation and cover crops, to a goal of 1:1.

I carry all these water thoughts to our own gardens that need a drink. I reluctantly drag the garden hose across our dried-up yard to the garden. We have long used up the collected rainwater that drains from our gutters into rain barrels. It seems that we need to do this more than ever this year. Water. Rain. These simple words weigh on my mind. It makes me question the six o'clock weather reporter who is always trying to put a spin on the forecasts with a preference for sunny days, where rain won't ruin your weekend plans. Are we really that out of touch? We need rain. When did we start thinking precipitation would ruin our day? All these thoughts circulate in my mind and raise my level of gratitude for any rainy-day forecasts. For when the rains finally came days later, I went outside and raised my hands to the cool drops hitting my face of relief and rejoiced, "*Wopida, wopida, wopida!*"

❖   ❖   ❖   ❖

Pizza Sauce

8 quarts peeled chopped tomatoes
2 teaspoons olive oil
2 cups chopped onions
1 bulb garlic, peeled and chopped
2 tablespoons dried basil
2 teaspoons fennel seeds
1/8 cup canning salt
1 teaspoon pepper
1/4 cup sugar
1 tablespoon dried oregano
1/2 teaspoon red pepper flakes
1 tablespoon dried thyme

Blanch tomatoes so that you can peel skins from them (blanching involves immersing in boiling water for a minute or two and then in ice-cold water). Use an Amish paste or similar tomato. Chop and mash tomatoes and put in a nonstick pot. On medium heat, bring tomatoes to a simmer and continue to cook, stirring often. In skillet, add oil and when hot, add onions and stir. When onions are near translucent, add garlic. Stir for a minute and add to tomatoes. Add remaining ingredients and turn heat to maintain a low simmer, stirring often so sauce does not burn. Cook for at least an hour, or longer to produce a thick pizza sauce. You could also add tomato paste to create a thicker sauce. Fill sterilized pint jars, leaving ½-inch headspace. Add a couple of drops of commercially bottled lemon juice. Process for 35 minutes in hot water bath.

IMPERFECT YET SPLENDID

Ceremony is not perfect, though it might be the process of mitigating the gap between sacredness and me and all that is incomplete, imperfect, and inconsolable. Through sacred acts and splendid gestures, there can still be pain and even loss. And so it is in the gardening rites and rituals as well.

The *su* or seed is complete, holding nearly all that it needs. It is just right with all the genetic properties stored in its tiny house to grow many offspring. Yet my engagement with seeds is not without flaw. Through trial and error, I have learned the timing of sowing seeds is critical. I cannot put seeds in the ground too early nor too late—too early and they rot; too late and they never have enough time to mature and produce offspring. Where I plant a seed also matters. Soils in many places have become depleted, leaving a seed to grow in empty dirt, void of the nutrients it needs, like nitrogen. It might even fool me into believing the soil is adequate, growing a plant but never any fruits, perhaps because it lacks phosphorous. Then there is consistent moisture that each seed and plant require, approximately one inch of rain per week. Mother Nature doesn't always follow this guideline, and conditions are even less predictable with changes in our climate. Thus, I have had to water freshly planted seeds, seedlings, and plants across our garden. In doing this, I have accidently drowned my plants, which is evident in their yellow appearance. They have also died of thirst, scorching from early heat in the prairie sun. But the more I practice planting and nurturing each seed, the deeper I experience the sacredness in our ceremonial exchange.

CHERISHED MOMENTS

One of my favorite summer evening activities is to spend time in the garden with Jay. I do not know if he knows this, and I am not even sure what aspect of being in the garden with him brings me joy. This evening after supper we are both milling around outside. As he enters the garden area he says, "Mama, you will have to check out the apple trees." I am bent over picking strawberries, and he goes on to tell me he will pick the strawberries. He is trying to help me with my arthritic knees, but in just a few minutes he exclaims that the strawberries need a few more days. He knows by now that I will not heed his indirect message but will continue bending over because by the time I am done, I have gathered at least two cups of berries. Had I waited two more days as he suggested, the few berries would have rotted, drawing in insects. Certainly, this small amount gathered is not enough to do much with but fresh berries on a bowl of ice cream are divine. He gives up and shortly after, I hear the four-wheeler. I am momentarily a little sad thinking of the motorized toy my husband, who is in his sixties, is driving around for entertainment. Images resurface of our boys cruising on the trails all summer long during their childhood days. I sigh and move on to pick some greens. One year, I left the various lettuces go to seed and found that they reseeded themselves and I now have an abundance of regenerative greens. My bowl is overflowing now with varied shades of greens, oak-shaped, dark maroon lettuce leaves, and beautiful green leaves with mottled, maroon-colored specks. Content with my early summer night's harvest, I follow Jay's suggestion, taking my time to marvel at the tiny green formations of apples. Once inside,

I run the sink with cold water and add the greens. Later, once the dirt has settled to the bottom of the sink, I will run them through a salad spinner. Then I will drop them on a clean kitchen towel to dry just a bit before packaging them into gallon bags with a paper towel to draw any remaining moisture. This methodical process will result in a couple of weeks of fresh greens.

I move on to clean up the handful of asparagus stalks and add them to yesterday's pick and sit down to destem the strawberries. I am nearly done when he plops down on the couch and asks where the ice cream is. I explain that I am nearly done preparing the berries. By the time he comes up from taking a shower, I hand him a bowl of ice cream topped with fresh berries, "Here you go, Daddy." We settle into our comfortable spots and watch the current series that consumes our evening interest. I cherish these simple evenings.

RECLAIMING

As part of the work that Dakota Wicoȟaŋ, a Native nonprofit dedicated to language and lifeways revitalization, has done, I recognize that the revitalization of Indigenous languages has been about reclaiming. After damaging assimilation policies, the Dakota language—this land's language—was on the brink of extinction. The language was, in fact, assaulted, damaged, and nearly eradicated. And in some ways, we as well. We, along with many others, work to restore the language, and no, we are not there yet: the work includes healing and restoring ourselves. Through this era of reclaiming language, traditions, and our very identities, I am also reclaiming myself—a Dakota *wiŋyaŋ* (woman).

In their book, *Reclaiming Youth at Risk*, authors Larry K. Brendtro, Martin Brokenleg, and Steve Van Bockern (2002) describe reclaiming as "to recover and redeem, to restore value to something that has been devalued." They discuss the way we as Indigenous peoples have raised and cared for our children. It is a call for the restoration of our humanity—of ourselves. I like to also think this is true with our relationship to *Ina Maka*. We have an opportunity to remember, reclaim, and reconnect to the land who provides and cares for us. When I get down close to her, dig my fingers and press my feet and toes into cool soils, I begin to restore that sacred memory and connection between us. When I walk amongst her in the woods, along the banks, and in the tall grass prairies, I begin to remember my connection to place, to nature, to creation. Reclaiming a connection between us, I begin to know and understand that I am a part of her and she is within me. As I continue to practice behaviors that reflect and honor *makoce kiŋ* (the land) as a cherished relative, the one that feeds me and sustains me, I understand that I am also being restored.

HARD WORK AND SACRIFICES

Hard work and sacrifice are a common thread among farmers, food producers, and gardeners. They commit to long hours of arduous work, and in the end there is no guarantee everything will work out. My brother and I can attest to the hard work growing up on the farm, yet now as an adult, I know my dad worked ten times harder than the rest of us put together. My dad, a navy veteran, left a good-paying job in the Twin Cities as a tool and die maker to take up farming. Dad bought the farm and 140 acres of land in the late 1970s, when land prices were high. We raised hogs, with Dad selling primarily feeder pigs and butcher hogs—not like the factory farms of today. I recall Dad wrestling with those pigs when it was time to load them up and understand now why his hands hurt from arthritis. There were also butcher chickens in the coop and a few head of cattle in the pasture behind the barn (one end of the pasture was mainly a wetlands area). On the fields Dad grew corn and soybeans, beholden to the commodity markets. I remember different times he'd have me listen to WCCO-AM for the farmer's market at noon on the little black radio in the kitchen. I would jot down the prices of feeder pigs so he could decide when he should sell. From Sarah K. Mock's book *Farm (and*

My oldest son, Hunter, at the farm of my childhood.

Other F Words), I learned that these commodity prices are really based on large-scale production and that typically the prices end up right where most farmers just break even. There might be some that will make a little more and others a little less. Dad recalled a year the corn prices were very low, at two dollars per bushel. He refused to sell at that significant loss and thought prices would go up. He ended up selling his bin full of corn at a dollar/bushel. He said that was a real low time in his farming. Only recently he revealed that story to me and said it was one of a couple of times we nearly went under—meaning we would have lost the farm. During the farm crisis when many farmers did lose their farms, he shared that some started shooting the bankers out of sheer desperation. During Dad's retirement phase, he took his time and sold chunks of land for people wanting to build rural homes. That income paid off any remaining farm debt, with more to invest later in the few acres of land and the house where Mom and Dad currently live. Overall, he said he proved a farmer didn't have to have thousands of acres to make it. Of course, we lived a contented, resourceful, and frugal lifestyle. Dad was devoted to the land, the animals, and a way of life that provided home-grown foods and a little income. Dad is nearly eighty now and he continues this approach to life by growing a garden, hunting, and fishing, and cutting wood for heat. He is satisfied by simple living.

I will admit there are times I wonder if the amount of work we put in each year is worth it. Let's take, for example, peas. I could just as easily purchase canned or frozen peas from the grocery store for a few dollars—a commodity food—uniform and cheap. Yet, here is what we do to gain two-gallon bags of frozen peas. Every other year, in the spring, Jay moves a fence and the posts to a new spot to plant the peas. During the alternate year, we will grow beans on this fence and plant peas in another area. He breaks up the ground enough so that I can go behind and place each pea about an inch deep in the ground. I plant them thick, about four peas deep as they are competitive. In other words, the more pea plants, the more aggressively they grow and produce peas. I do this on both sides of the fence, which can take some time. Then in early summer they are ready to start picking. They will pro-duce for a few weeks and then they are done. At first, you will only pick a handful. These I typically just eat fresh while in the garden. Soon, they will produce enough for a tiny serving with our meal. Then suddenly, you have enough to start freezing. A vigilant eye is required, as pea pods are the same color of green as the plants. No matter how many times I go back, I seem to find more. Then there is the shelling and I like to sit with a couple of bowls while watching television. Memory will provide a familiar rhythm and pattern where I know one side of the pea pod is easier to snap open and run my thumb along the inside of the pod to easily pluck each pea from its tiny, short string that attaches itself to the pod. In no time, I will have two cups of peas. Only two cups? you ask. Yes, but imagine doing this every or every other day for a couple of weeks. Each day gets you closer to filling that freezer bag. But wait, you cannot just freeze raw peas. Once my shelling is complete, then I get a pot of water boiling and dump the peas in. Leave them in for less than two minutes. You do not fully cook them. They should still be bright green and somewhat firm and not that gray-green color and mushy feel of canned peas. You then drain the peas through a strainer and quickly add them to ice cold water, which stops them from cooking further. This process is called blanching and is intended to kill the enzyme, as my *kuŋśi* used to describe to me when blanching sweet corn for drying. Okay, time for the science, which I actually had to look up because I just trust Grannie's words. Blanching, which is done with boiling water, inactivates the enzyme and destroys microorganisms that might contaminate the vegetables. There are other ways besides hot-water blanching, including microwaving, steam, and infrared blanching. Enzymes left to do their work slowly deteriorate the fruit's or vegetable's flavor, color, odor, and nutritional value. This all makes more sense about why eating vegetables right out of the garden provides optimal nutrition. After the cold-water rinse, I put the peas on a clean dish towel and shake them around. I make sure that I have the towel secured so that peas are not escaping and rolling onto the floor getting contaminated. Then I spread them on a cookie sheet, ensuring they are no more than single layered. Then I put the whole sheet in the freezer for a couple of hours. If you skip the step of drying the peas a bit, the remaining water can cause them to freeze together in big clumps. I use a metal spatula to gently scrape up the peas from the cookie sheet and scoop them into a freezer bag. Then I have my own freezer peas throughout the year to use in cold macaroni salads, tuna noodle hotdish, vegetable soups, and cooked to serve as a side vegetable.

I recall one year some time back the peas were looking lush and just full of white blossoms as they raced to the top. I was filled with excitement, knowing I would have an abundant harvest. That was until one morning as I walked the garden grounds, the peas on the side of the fence facing the prairie grass were mowed down nearly to the ground. All the delicate flowers that had scattered up their vines across the whole width and length of the fence were absent, and what remained were green stems and some of the oval ruffled petals. That was the year I told Jay he better slay me the deer responsible for gorging on my hard work. It was also the same year I asked my dad to help me build an electric fence. My oldest son, Hunter, converted it to a solar-powered fence the following year.

Deer aren't the only ones who have mowed down the peas. I recall a particular time, *Icepaƞśi* (Cousin) Gaby came over for a visit while I was out in my garden. She joined me on one side of the pea fence while I gathered from the other. We had just a fantastic time catching up on the goings-on across our communities and families. Yet soon I noticed I was farther down the fence, making it harder for conversation. Did I mention peapods are hard to find? Green on green is a good camouflage. I figured Gaby was just having trouble finding them, and so I joined her on the other side of the fence to help her finish gathering pods. Once we were done, I poured her pods, which looked quite sparse, with mine into a recycled bag. We continued our visit as we walked back down the pathway, which seemed to be littered with empty pods. True, that day I had far less than my usual amount to freeze. But the oohing and ahhing from friends and family is one of the greatest joys of growing food. I imagine that my fellow farmers, food producers, and gardeners are fortified by similar joys.

✦   ✦   ✦   ✦

Tuna Noodle Hotdish

1 bag egg noodles
1 cup milk
1 can cream of mushroom or cream of celery soup
2 5-ounce cans of tuna in water
2 cups frozen or freshly picked peas
1 cup crushed potato chips

Cook noodles al dente, rinse, and set aside. In a large bowl, combine the milk and soup; whisk until creamy. Strain water from cans of tuna and add. Pour peas into mix. Next add cooked pasta and stir. I like to butter the inside of a baking dish before pouring in the noodle mix. Season with pepper. Cover and bake at 350 for 45 minutes. Remove cover, sprinkle crushed potato chips over casserole. Bake uncovered for 10 more minutes. We traditionally eat this with buttered bread. Because I am known to be resourceful, I make this dish when there is a neglected bag of chips because what remains is two inches of chip crumbs— too tedious for Jay to eat and far too much to throw away.

RECIPROCITY

Each year we gather an abundance of gifts from our plant relatives. There is a long list of fruits and vegetables harvested throughout the season, all in their own time. Most are from those we plant and nurture from our own garden space. Yet, some are gathered beyond—in the woods, on hillsides, and along local waterways. We forage wild foods and medicines, including *wicahdeśka* (goose-berries), *kaŋta* (plums), *hastaŋhaŋka* (grapes), *caŋpa* (chokecher-ries), *tukiha* (shells), *ḣaŋte* (cedar), and *pejiḣota* (sage). The plant relatives give freely, nourishing our physical and spiritual vessels, and those of friends and family. In turn, my responsibility is to be a respectful relative. Robin Wall Kimmerer shares guidelines for an "Honorable Harvest": asking permission, taking only what you need, leaving some for others (in my mind, this includes the birds), harvesting in a way that minimizes harm, never wasting what you have taken, sharing, giving thanks, and giving a gift for what you have taken.

We too follow these guidelines, and while no one in particular ever instructed us to do so, I believe that when we are in relation-ship with the land and all that she offers, honoring these unoffi-cial guidelines becomes quite natural. For example, chokecherries have always been a traditional and spiritual food and medicine among Dakota people. As such, we expect to return year after year to harvest them, and so we will be careful not to harm the bush and branches. Sometimes the berries are plentiful and other years less so—this causes me not to take them for granted but to appreciate them fully. And clusters of the tiny wild grapes, much smaller than store-bought grapes, are foraged from the valleys of the Wakpamnisota (Minnesota River) to make oh-so-deliciously tart wild grape jelly so incredible you will want to share it!

Back in my garden, my responsibility may look a bit different—yet a relationship is still evident. I tend to the plants by gingerly pulling out "weeds" next to each plant that are taking away needed nutrients and water. During dry spells, we have the extra labor of hauling buckets of rainwater from the barrel near the garden shed and dragging the hose from our house to the garden. Muddy and bug-bitten after the hours it takes to quench the thirst of all the plants across our garden, I am even more grateful each time it rains amidst this seemingly unprecedented drought. Tending the plants includes checking on their readiness and assessing the ripeness of their fruits and vegetables. I caress my hands across plant leaves but intuitively hear "not yet." I gently tap the hot pepper plants, causing them to release their hotness, or so I have been told by other gardeners. I readjust the mulch of grass clippings, dried leaves, and straw around the plants, while poking my finger into the soil to gauge moisture levels. Then there is the excitement and gratitude as I gather first harvests, seconds and thirds as my veggie and fruit freezer begins to refill. The birds too—they are eating insects and providing song to me, their melodies encouraging me and nurturing my spirit as I bend, stretch, and lean over Mother Earth—she who takes care of us. This is a big circle joining the land, plants, animal nations, and me—a circle of relationships and the gifting among us. Reciprocity and a harmonious give-and-take happen among us relatives.

One day I spent considerable time operating on the *Gete-okosomin*, which I understand means "cool old squash" in the Ojibwe language. This squash is originally from the Miami tribe of Indiana and Ohio and was gifted amongst several people before my happy receipt. The squash *is* pretty cool—it is long and bright orange with thick rinds, and just one can feed several people. The operation I was performing was in the hope of saving the plants from the fatal squash borers. Other years it is the squash bugs that I battle. I look up squash bug and squash borer in the Dakota dictionary and sure enough we have words for them—*wabduśkazizi* and *oŋ oḣdogyapi.* I thought for sure the squash bugs were from another planet, but no—they have been here right along with my Indigenous relatives! I wonder what our ancestors did to save their squash crop from these devastating insects. I slit open the main stem of its core after clearing as much soil away, careful not to expose too much of its roots. I dig around with my knife and search for the fat white larvae with what looks like one big black eye of a cyclops. "Come here, you sucker," I pant through my attempts, as it recoils from the sharp of my blade. What is the reciprocity in this? I wonder. They seem to just be taking—gorging on the essence of the squash, the life force found within the core of the squash. With some of the squash stems I dig two or three out and even find some baby larvae. I do this quickly so as not to keep the buried core out in the sun for too long. I rebury the stem and add more soil, patting them into a mound. I look for another good spot along the vine to mound up a pile of dirt so that there is a chance the little hairs on the vine might turn into roots. I do this across ten plants, getting up off the ground all dirty from sitting on my *oŋze* because my knees won't bend for a squat. Yet, I am thankful for the hyaluronic acid the doctor injected into both, allowing me to work longer in the garden than I was able to earlier in the year. I thought about leaving each of the wriggling larvae out for the birds to eat but I couldn't chance it, I sliced each one in half and occasionally would smash them with a nearby rock, some even with my fingers. Earlier, we had battled cucumber beetles during their mating season. They were found in the abundant yellow blossoms of the southwest melon vines. These I am trying to grow from seeds gifted to me by our Pueblo friend and fellow gardener, Shkeme. We still are battling them but have them under control. I read that a plant can lose up to 25 percent of its foliage before the threat of dying. Yes, just like people, plants have a strong will to live.

Later that afternoon, post surgery, I head to the garden again to take a look at the squash vines. They are wilted and suffering. I ask Jay to water them gently with the sprinkler so as not to knock off the soil I mounded on their stems. He mutters something and then tells me, "I wouldn't do what you are doing. You should stop growing them." The next morning, they look better, perked up, and I am grateful. I will watch over them for the next few days, hoping and praying they will make it. There are several finger-like yellow squashes forming throughout all of them. I pray my efforts will come to fruition. If successful, they hold up well for winter storage. However, I also just like taking a day and cooking them and freezing the roasted meat in quart bags. When roasting them, it is easier to put them on a cookie sheet and cook them whole. Then we slice them open and gut the stringy insides and seeds after they are done roasting. But if I am able, on a very patient day, I cut one open before cooking and remove the seeds to save for another year. Yes, maybe in the following years I will give up on planting these sisters in my garden to see if the squash bugs move away. Note that I say, my garden—as I have plans for the yards of my sons' nearby homes.

Following the operation day, while I was in the garden, a small snake startled me. I was walking away from the raspberries and it was slithering toward the berries. I assumed it is the same little garter that scared me weeks earlier when I was weeding onions in a nearby raised bed. It was nestled under the dried leaves I had placed in the bed between the onions and carrots to keep the weeds down and moisture in. It had peeked its head out, looking at me and tasting my essence, its tongue moving in and out. Its curious eyes looked at me, unafraid. Which is why it appeared to me that it was casually passing me by as it made its way into the cool lanes of raspberries—like we were common acquaintances. I was thinking that evening of our encounter and wondered where it was going and what its intention was. Maybe it tasted the essence of the three little bird eggs I found in the farthest raspberry row. Weeks earlier, I had discovered a half-built nest. More recently the nest was nicely formed and move-in ready. Then as the raspberries were winding down their abundant crop, three grayish-blue ovals appeared in the nest. It seemed as if the mother knew my daily routine of disturbing the area was becoming less often, thus it was safe to build a nest. That morning I had gathered only a handful of berries, just enough for my morning breakfast. Curious and a bit worried, I went back out that night to check on the eggs. I was convinced I would see an empty nest or at least a missing egg—a healthy meal for our slithery garden acquaintance, or shall I say relative? But to my surprise they were all still there. Had the little reptile just gone in to find shade? Or perhaps it had been only looking to gorge on the oodles of mos-

Nest of bird eggs in the raspberry patch.

quitoes and insects that left itchy bite marks all over my legs and back during the two weeks of prime berry picking? I settled on it being a mutually beneficial exchange, a complementary gifting between the garter, berries, insects, and me.

✦   ✦   ✦   ✦

Squash Boats

1 *Gete-okosomin* squash
1 pound buffalo burger
1 onion, chopped
2 garlic cloves, minced
1 jar salsa
2 cups cooked rice
8 ounces shredded cheddar cheese
sliced jalapeños

This recipe is inspired by my friend Mary Jo. With a heavy knife, cut the squash in half and scoop out the seeds and stringy pulp. Save and clean the seeds—some for seed saving and some for

recipe continued ▶

roasting. Place the squash upside down on a cookie sheet lined
with parchment paper. Bake for at least one hour at 350, until
fork tender (depending upon size, baking time may take longer).
While the squash is baking, fry buffalo burger with onion and
garlic. Add a jar of salsa and mix. Fold in rice. Top baked squash
with burger mix, add cheese, and finish with jalapenos. Bake
15 more minutes until cheese is melted. Cut into hearty slabs.

This can be modified with various ingredients, including rice
and beans.

BELIEF

"Mom! Those are women's signs of a heart attack or stroke." My
mom had casually recounted to me the symptoms she had the
day before—chest pain, burning in the throat, nausea, sweat, and
chills. My sense of urgency did not motivate her to go straight to
the hospital as I hoped. Yet she did commit to telling her oncologist, whom she would be seeing the following Monday. The
oncologist, of course sent her to a cardiologist, who diagnosed
her with heart disease—clogged arteries. Mom was scheduled
for an angiogram and stent procedure the following Monday.
She would be home in plenty of time before Jay and I left for a
Montana vacation, years in the planning. I am familiar with stent
procedures because my dad has had the procedure twice. During
a stent procedure, the doctor inserts a tiny tube in a main artery,
often through the groin area. Dye released into the bloodstream
reveals where the blockages are that are slowing blood flow to the
heart. A tiny balloon pushes the plaque to the walls of the artery,
widening it. The stent, which looks like part of a ballpoint pen,
is inserted and the balloon deflated, creating space for increased
blood flow. I understand that this is a common procedure with
minimal risk. My dad was out of the hospital the following day
each time.

That mid-Monday morning, Dad called me with the news.
Mom would not have the common stent procedure as planned.
She would actually require open-heart surgery. Holy cow! The

next day, we met with a different doctor—the kind of doctor who specializes in bypasses. His drawing showed the main arteries in front of her heart were 95 percent blocked and another at 70 percent. She would need a triple bypass. It was quite serious. But Mom in her typical casual fashion and without any family discussion said, "Let's do it." The doctors kept her in the hospital, monitoring her heart and blood pressure, conducting numerous tests, and preparing her for the scheduled operation on Thursday morning.

The day before surgery, Dad advised me to come to the hospital in the morning whenever I woke up—meaning, sleep as long as you like; her surgery would be a long one. Tossing and turning most of the night, I ignored Dad's instructions. I got up very early, quickly cleaned up, and was out the door with a cup of coffee by 4:30 a.m. I understood that I wouldn't likely make it to the hospital in time to see her before they wheeled her down to pre-op at 6:30 a.m., but at least I could be there with Dad until she was wheeled back up into the intensive care unit (ICU) early afternoon. Despite road construction and parking challenges, I made it to her room just before they wheeled her out. I was so relieved, as they pushed back pre-op to 7:00 a.m.! Dad and I followed the rolling gurney and entourage of nurses. Pre-op was in the basement, where more medical staff came to prepare her for the operation. I learned that this one-hour time-out is a newer medical practice to ensure correct patient and procedure. This made sense as I see a lineup of curtains and patient stations down both sides of the walls. A lot of commotion took up much of this final hour, but finally we had a few silent moments with her. Then suddenly it was time, and my mind went blank. I had no good words to express to her. Certainly, we all knew the potential risks with cutting someone open, stopping one's heart, having machines function on your behalf, all while the doctor cuts and pulls arteries from your leg and other parts of your body to create an alternative route for your blood to pass through. More afraid to not say anything before this incredibly scary procedure, I grabbed her hand and said, "Ma, I'll see you upstairs in a few hours."

Dad and I took our time finding the way to the surgery family waiting room, then getting breakfast and coffee, visiting, looking at our phones and clocks, and sitting in silence. If it weren't for the periodic family updates, I am quite sure one would go mad. They gave us three updates during the nearly six-hour wait. We were most relieved during the last update when they restarted her heart and were sewing her up. We could now move to the fourth floor to the ICU family waiting room. We had another two-hour wait while they got her situated, then we could finally see her. The doctor warned us that she would look a bit rough. While she did have the typical pale puffy face they described, still the sight of her stunned us. There were so many tubes coming out of her, including the ventilator tube that distorted her mouth and ran down her throat to her lungs to keep her breathing. But mainly what I wasn't prepared for was the absence of her presence. If she were merely dozing, I could rouse her from sleep and she would ask, "What?!" Yet, Dad and I both talked to her as if she was just napping. "Ma, you did a good job. Time to wake up now." Later, with a bit more agency, I added, "Ma, you got to take some breaths now. They won't pull the ventilator out until you do." The ICU crew would work to decrease her sedation, then wait for her to start waking up. The nurses would work to calm her as she would lift her hands toward her mouth in slow motion. She was starting to gag on the tube down her throat. I can't imagine the discomfort! All of us took turns reminding her she needed to breathe on her own before they would take the ventilator tube out. The process was taking longer than expected. While her oxygen levels would improve through her breath intake, her carbon dioxide levels were still too high. She was not exhaling adequately. This cycle would go on until the evening shift nurse kicked us out. The ICU visitor hours were long past. While both of us were discouraged, it was Dad who expressed grave concern. "I'm not worried, Dad. They said it happens. Some people just need more time to breathe on their own," I replied. "I don't believe them," Dad quickly retorted. "It's not her time, Dad," I quietly added. With nothing more to say, Dad walked across the street from the hospital to family housing, and

I made the drive home. I called the ICU as soon as I entered the house and was told it was early in the repeated cycle. "She's just coming off of sedation, and we'll check her levels again." I vowed I would call early in the morning.

I woke up after another night of limited sleep. Feeling confident, though, I made coffee, sat down, and called the number I had now memorized. "Hi, this is Joyce's daughter. Can you put me through to her nurse?" As I listened to the updated report on my mom, I burst into unexpected tears. The nurse shared that yes, Mom was now off the ventilator. It took until two in the morning but yes, she's breathing on her own. What a relief!

After calling and assuring Dad that she was finally off the ventilator, he in turn reassured me that yes, we should continue with our vacation plans. Mom would be in the hospital for some time yet, with doctors and nurses tending to her needs. Yet we were prepared to cancel had Mom not started breathing on her own. A few hours later, our middle son, Tanner, drove us to the Twin Cities. Relief and excited energy filled the car as we exhaled, releasing anxiety and fear. He dropped us off in front of the Delta departure sign, and ninety minutes later we were boarding our plane to Billings, Montana.

Every winter for several consecutive years, I would declare a future fallow garden year so that I could check something off my "bucket list." But year after year I would get the spring planting itch and proclaim, "Next year, we'll go next year." After taking a full-time job this past January, and with declined energy levels, I announced that this would be the year for a Montana road trip. Consequently, I made plans for a seriously scaled-back garden.

Scaled-back plans still included at least a tomato plant or two for slicers. So, I took the extra time and resources to plant a mere twenty tomato seeds and a dozen pepper seeds. All the seeds sprouted, sprung their seed leaves, and even their tiny true leaves began emerging. But then, something happened that has never happened in all my years seeding plants. All of the plants stayed small. They never grew beyond the delicate stems and tiny leaves. We kept asking what was happening and wondered why they wouldn't grow. I kept them under the lights despite realizing they had stopped growing. Eventually, I moved them outdoors, just as if I were weaning them. I even went so far as to plant them and fortified their planting holes with bone meal and fertilizer. But in just a few days, the infant plants had all but disappeared into the soil. Jay questioned if I had done something wrong. Perhaps the seeds were too old, or I used the wrong soil. But I knew why. My original intention and ultimately the lack of faith is what stunted their growth. I decided then that whatever was planted in the garden this year would receive its due care, but I detached from any expectations.

Part of the due diligence of care includes watering. I purchased a few soaker hoses and snaked them next to the few things I did plant—carrots, green beans, and onions just to make it a little easier. Jay still scolded me more than once: "I thought you said we weren't gardening this year." He still supported me and watered the plants I managed to sneak in, including two tomato plants and one pepper plant a fellow garden friend gifted me, after I shared my self-fulfilling prophetic story. Of course, too, there was still the garlic I planted last fall and the perennials that needed adequate watering during the fruiting period—strawberries, raspberries, blackberries, and aronia berries. We left instructions with my middle son, Hepaŋna, who stayed while we were gone. The list I left didn't include watering plants, I asked that he pick the green beans as they would stop producing if left unpicked. He graciously house-, dog-, and cat-sat for us while we spent that week in Montana.

We flew into Billings abundant with faith. We trusted that Mom would continue to recover, and she would be back home by the time we would return home. We held confidence that *Hepaŋna* would manage the house, garden, and our furry family members. I kept these beliefs as we toured across Big Sky Country. We hit most of the places we had spent months planning for, including Glacier National Park (GNP). The park would be the pinnacle of our trip. The national park had decided this would be the year to pilot a new program, limiting the number of vehicles in the park—an effort in environmental protection. I had Jay call the

1–800 number while I maneuvered through the website. We were both praying one of us would score a treasured ticket. In just a few minutes, I was able to put a vehicle ticket in my "cart," when Jay handed the phone to me to talk with the lady on the phone. I recognized her voice as the same who had explained the pilot strategy to me months ago. My fingers paused impatiently on the keyboard while I gave her my name, address, and all the other required information. Challenged with trying to do both strategies at the same time, I reluctantly assured myself that she worked for the park and certainly wouldn't be asking for our information if she couldn't secure a ticket. "Minnesota, 56214," I answered. I could hear her tapping in my responses on her keyboard. "Okay, mm-hmm," she replied. "Oh, sorry, the tickets are already sold out." What?! How could this be? We had spent far less time trying to get a ticket than the twenty minutes she had warned me it would take before they would sell out. Taking a deep breath, I explained to her that I was working through the online process at the same time, as she had suggested. But now, it asked for a password. She promised to send me a reset email before we ended the call. She assured me we could try tomorrow. With a big disappointed sigh, I worked to accept that we wouldn't be going to GNP tomorrow. I looked down at my open laptop in defeat. I might as well check my email for that reset password so that I would be ready for tomorrow's effort. I opened the national park email and clicked on the icon to reset the password. Upon clicking enter, the site brought me back to my "cart." Holy! The vehicle ticket was still there! Is that possible? I completed the process and exclaimed, "Honey, I did it. We are going to Glacier tomorrow!"

Now headed north, we passed through the lands of the Confederated Salish and Kootenai Tribes of the Flathead Nation. We motored along in our rental around the perimeter of Flathead Lake—a remnant glacier lake with depths reaching 370 feet! Our breath was taken away by the scenery. We reached our final destination, the city of Kalispell, late afternoon. Jay went golfing again while I rested in our hotel room and scanned map routes, thankful that we would be able to get into the park.

In the morning, we loaded up with water and snacks and were on the road by 8:00 a.m. One of our first stops was overlooking Lake McDonald. The lake was iridescent and spectacular, resembling aqua aura quartz stones or the abalone earrings hanging on my bedroom dresser. Another stop brought us to a secret mountain stream babbling over glacier stones, boulders, and felled cedars and cottonwoods. The hills and valleys tempered any human sounds. All that I could hear were songs from nearby birds and the mountain stream rushing and bubbling over rocks and pebbles, smoothing any sharp edges along its path. I sat down on a rock, removed my Keens, and put my bare feet in the chilly mountain water. I looked up at Jay with tears in my eyes and said, "The birds are so happy. This is so incredible I could cry." And then I did. It took us the entire day to travel the famous Going-to-the-Sun Road. There were melting glaciers, never-ending waterfalls, and more trees than our eyes could take in. My breathing quickened as we drove around curves, sometimes so close to the mountain edges that revealed death to anyone who veered from the narrow pathways. The road continued around Saint Mary Lake and looped back around to the west entrance. Each stop was a spectacular and unique view of splendor. It was a full day of traveling through the park and worth every minute.

Our flight and drive home took all day, too. But unlike the day before, the views lacked interest, much less beauty. Pavement, crowds and lines of people, smells of jet fuel, fast food, and blaring cars speeding by filled my senses. I couldn't wait to return to our sanctuary. On the plane and drive home, I thought about the splendor and magic of the park. And then began to recall the beauty in our own river valley. How might we honor the beautiful spaces and sanctuaries in our own back yard?

Home again! My own bed. While we enjoy traveling from time to time, we are always filled with gratitude upon our return home. Perhaps it is the few steps needed for a good cup of coffee. Or maybe it's the longing for homemade food after too many fast-food choices. A strong desire for plainness emerges after just a few days—buttered toast, a fried egg, a piece of fruit. Then, of course,

I rest at a secret mountain stream in Glacier National Park.

there is the garden. I immediately absorb the near silence, speckled with the simple sounds of a few birds, Rasta's sniffing, and leaves rustling from a light wind. I breathe in the warm morning air and start. I pick a big bowl of green beans and a cake pan of overripe raspberries. I pull a few onions, searching for the ones that won't result in keepers and walk into the house. I decide on tomorrow's menu based on my harvest: green bean soup, jalapeño and cheddar zucchini bread, and zucchini brownies.

After I clean up, I drive a mere eight miles north. Dropping down first, then winding up the hill and out of the valley, and then west over to my parents' home. I place a bag of souvenirs on the deck. Mom shuffled out with her new four-legged companion—a walker to support her labored steps. Dad followed her closely, hand on the back of her elbow, his eyes glued on her until she sat down on the lawn chair. We discuss her progress and remark over how she is only taking Tylenol for pain. She shows me the vertical zigzag scar traveling down her chest—still red and swollen. I ask to look at the place where they took her artery from her leg. She shows me the small red slit on the upper part of her bruised-up leg. Actually, her whole body appears bruised. But for the most part, she looks and sounds like Mom. "Mom, you gave us quite a scare."

Green Bean Soup with Dumplings

3 cups fresh green beans, chopped
bacon, chopped, or ham hock
1 medium onion, chopped
3 garlic cloves, chopped
2 tablespoons butter
chicken broth + water
pepper

Dumplings
2 cups flour
1 teaspoon salt
1 tablespoon baking powder
2 tablespoons oil
1 cup warm water

On medium heat, fry chopped bacon in Dutch oven. I used a half pound of left-over bacon. A ham bone, ham, Canadian bacon, or pork hock could be used in lieu of bacon. Push cooked bacon to the side and add onion, using the remaining bacon grease to fry onion. Season with pepper. When nearly translucent, add garlic. Stir and add butter. Stir and add green beans. Season with pepper. Add about 6 cups of a combination of chicken broth and water. Cover pot. Make dumplings: mix dry ingredients together, add oil and water, mix well but do not overmix. Let sit for 20 minutes. Drop spoonfuls of dumpling mix into pot and cover immediately; simmer for at least 15 minutes. This recipe is inspired by my late stepgrandpa Harvey and my German heritage.

Jalapeño Cheddar Zucchini Bread

2 cups shredded zucchini
2 cups flour
2 teaspoons baking powder
½ teaspoon baking soda

$^1/_2$ teaspoon salt
1 cup milk + 1 tablespoon white vinegar
1 egg
3 tablespoons melted butter
1 cup shredded cheddar cheese
$^1/_4$ cup chopped jalapeños

Clean zucchini and remove ends. If not too big, shred entire zucchini in processor. If overgrown with a tough skin and mature seeds, remove outer skin with peeler. Cut zuke in half and remove seeds. Shred remaining chunks. Mix dry ingredients in bowl and set aside. Stir milk and vinegar together or substitute buttermilk. Let the vinegar and milk set for a few minutes (it will look chunky or curdled). Mix egg, butter, and milk together. Stir in zucchini. Stir in flour mixture. Do not overmix. Gently stir in cheese and jalapeños. Pour into a greased 9-×-5-inch bread pan. Bake for 1 hour at 350 degrees. Check bread with a toothpick to be sure bread is done. Let cool. Bread is fantastic a day later toasted with a little butter.

Zucchini Brownies

2$^1/_2$ cups shredded zucchini
1$^1/_2$ cups sugar
$^1/_2$ cup oil
1 egg
1 tablespoon vanilla extract
2 cups flour
$^1/_4$ cup cocoa
1$^1/_2$ teaspoon baking soda
$^1/_2$ teaspoon salt

Prepare zucchini as described for the jalapeño cheddar zucchini bread. Combine zucchini, sugar, oil, egg, and vanilla. Mix dry ingredients and add to zucchini mix. Bake at 350 degrees in a greased 9-×-13-inch pan for 35 minutes.

Frosting
3 tablespoons butter
$^1/_2$ cup sugar
3 tablespoons milk

recipe continued ▶

½ teaspoon vanilla extract
½ cup semi-sweet or milk chocolate chips

Bring butter, sugar, and milk to a boil for 30 seconds. Remove from heat and add vanilla extract and chocolate chips. Stir. Let sit for a few minutes and frost cooled brownies. Double frosting if you desire a thick layer of frosting or use the rest for your next batch of brownies because where there's one zucchini, there's more!

RETURNING TO BALANCE

Scanning the plat map, I locate our 6.44 acres and it reads, "Jason Peterson, Et ux." This is where we live: Section 29:1, within the borders of the Swedes Forest Township. Upon looking up the meaning of "Et ux," I suddenly feel like a piece of property. It is Latin for "and wife." My mind quickly shifts to the patriarchal concept of ownership—land and chattel, like wife, children, livestock, and slaves. I shake the thought from my head. Jay doesn't own me, we are partners. We balance each other out. He runs hot, yet is calm, patient, and laid back, while I am wired a bit high strung and cool to the touch. He cleans the floors; I do the laundry. Spring and fall, he prepares the garden beds, and I plant, tend, and harvest. Through our partnership, I have been able to pursue and accomplish many things because he has supported me and kept me grounded. Our relationship is far from a traditional patriarchy but instead resembles the Dakota matriarchal form where the woman owns the lodge. For example, I typically make our financial and property decisions. Yet, our relationship is nontraditional, as he brought the patience needed as primary caregiver while I worked full-time when our boys were little. Yes, I would say we have a balanced bond, each contributing our gifts to the relationship, and bringing harmony throughout the seasons.

We have resided in this space together for twenty years or so. After closer examination of the abstract, I read the chronicle of prior owners of the original land. Each owner sold off parcels of land, bit by bit. Some of the names include Huseby, Knutson,

Christianson, Kannke, Stensvad, Olson, and Gimmestad, as well as easements to Redwood County and the Northern States Power Company. And finally, I come to the beginning of the document, "Pre-emption Patent dated August 5, 1869, of 80 acres. United States of America, By the President, U. S. Grant . . . Recorder of the General Land Office to John A. Willard."

The Homestead Act of 1862, signed by President Abraham Lincoln, provided settlers with 80 or 160 acres of "federal land"—land that had been stolen from or, at the very least, swindled from the Dakota and other Native peoples. Settlers were granted free and clear title after five years, or they could purchase the land outright for $1.25 per acre after living on and "improving" it for six months. Before 1862, larger sections of land, 640 and 320 acres, were sold to generate government income. But this strategy proved difficult owing to the significant labor needed to clear those larger sections. As I continue to read the National Archives' materials on the Homestead Act, I learn there was some public opposition to increased homesteading in the west for fear of the potential loss of cheap labor in eastern factories. Eventually, the Homestead Act provided the process for claiming land through an application and by making land improvements; after five years, one could file for a patent or deed to the land.

Owning land is a considerable asset for building wealth. I once heard that 25 percent of wealth in the United States can be directly tied back to the Homestead Act. This early government stimulus strategy, which was in effect from 1862 to 1904, was, in fact, land theft: more than 500 million acres of Native lands were taken. In her book *Farm (and Other F Words)*, Sarah Mock provides a description of the origins of wealth generation from homestead farms: "Our 'amber waves of grain' love affair with these farms is rooted in hundreds of years of white settler culture . . . the American Dream that encouraged white immigrants to take Indigenous land, enslave people to work it, and transform it into cash by whatever means necessary."

Of the more than 500 million acres of Native lands taken, 80 million acres (16 percent) actually went toward homesteads.

There were others who benefited through significant acts of fraud, including land speculators, miners, loggers, and railroad companies, which is where much of today's philanthropic wealth originates from. Yet, the original fraud centers the question, "How can these lands even be granted in the first place?" Only through coercion and outright theft.

U. S. Grant, the nation's eighteenth president, granted John A. Willard 80 acres of land in 1869 that rightfully belonged to my Dakota ancestors. Before Willard and Grant, this parcel of land was part of the northern end of the Mdewakaŋtoŋwaŋ and Waȟpekute treaty lands of 1851. It was part of a narrow strip on the southern side of the Wakpamnisota (the Minnesota River) and was all that remained of Dakota lands after several earlier land cession treaties—treaties that were never fully upheld by the government. This and subsequent events resulted in the war of 1862. After the six-week war, our Dakota ancestors were force marched and held in a concentration camp that winter at Fort Snelling. On that fateful and historic day of December 26, 1862, thirty-eight Dakota men were mass hanged in Maȟkato (Blue Earth; Mankato). To date, this is the largest mass execution in U.S. history. Others were imprisoned in Davenport, Iowa; women, children, and elderly prisoners were shipped to Crow Creek, South Dakota. And some, including my great-great-grandmother and her family, fled to Canada. In 1863, Congress abrogated all the treaties with the Dakota and exiled our people from their homelands.

Many years later, my great-great-grandmother Taṡina Susbeca Wiŋ, and her family, along with other Dakota people, made their way back to Mni Sota Makoce—Land of Cloudy Waters (note: there are other translations, however this is the one taught to me by my grandmother, who was in part raised by her grandmother, Taṡina Susbeca Wiŋ). Longing to return home, many of our people bought back some of their homelands. The irony they must have felt, knowing the history of what happened to their land and people. Today I wonder if those generations of families who claim pride in owning farmlands for more than a hundred years really know how those homesteads were gained. As for me, I feel a sense

Sunset on the Mni Sota Wakpa.

of resolute care and righteous belonging for the 6.44 acres now labeled as Section 29:1 within the borders of the Swedes Forest Township.

Before homesteads and reservations, before boundary lines, surveyors, and speculators—before treaties and land theft—this land was simply Dakota homelands. Mni Sota Makoce held *tioś-payes*, multigenerational and extended families of the Dakota *oyate* (nation or people). I think on these things as I walk across these lands and to the creek below us that is nestled within a coulee. It is a natural and perfect campsite for long-ago traveling Dakota. The creek is fed by the nearby Big Spring. Settlers had renamed it Boiling Spring because of the steam that rose from it in the winter. A marker just three hundred yards from our home, inscribed by the Redwood County Centennial Committee of 1862–1962, states that it "was long an Indian camping place and later a watering spot on the Fort Snelling-Dakota Road built in the 1850s."

Our home sits on top of a bluff overlooking the vast Minnesota River valley. Today this land is surrounded by homestead and corporate farmlands that each year predictably produce

Coneflower on our lands.

corn, soybeans, and sugar beets. This "progress" has garnered a limited diversity of plant life. I like to believe that the bees and pollinators prefer to gather at our diverse cornucopia of blossoms and nectar. Our lands are void of field corn, soybeans, and sugar beets and the accompanying chemicals that cause pollinating relatives to lose their internal compass. While we are planning to restore more, sections on our small plot hold reseeded prairie grasses—little bluestem, purple coneflower, black-eyed Susan, Indian grass, shooting star, yarrow, and more. All these plants help to maintain the blood memories of this landscape when land was treated as a relative. I think about how much change has occurred since the start of the Homestead Act to today's current capitalistic and extractive economy. How have these changes defined and shaped our daily decisions and choice of lifeways, including "feeding America" to farming our babies out to strangers to be raised by other mothers? These questions swirling in my mind are not meant to hold judgment over individual decisions but are directed toward the lack of choice and the capitalist system many feel trapped by. I am struck by the imbalance between a few with more than they will ever need and the vast majority, who are working hard to keep the "system" going while missing life's sweet moments.

I am back at the spring and listening to the sounds of the land and the company of relatives—bees and flies, butterflies and moths, grasshoppers and birds who also relish in the sounds of life. The spring's waters running year-round offer fresh water for deer, rabbits, coyotes, and other relatives. In the spring, even up the hill where our house sits, I can hear the fullness of the creek, though in the summer, less so with the thick foliage muffling the flow. The meandering path strewn with fallen leaves in the autumn invites me to sit in the quiet once again. And like many natural springs, despite frigid temperatures in the winter, she continues to flow surrounded by mounds of snow and patches of ice. Today, sitting on a felled tree near the spring, I decide that one small act to return to balance is to reclaim the spring's original name, Mni Ohdoka Taŋka, just as my relatives would have called it.

✦   ✦   ✦   ✦

Perfectly Balanced Succotash

1 small zucchini
1 small yellow or summer squash
1 teaspoon olive oil
1 onion
1 bell pepper
2 cloves garlic, finely chopped
1 large tomato, chopped
1 cup corn
1 teaspoon cumin
salt and pepper, to taste

Cube zucchini and squash and toss in heated oil in sauté pan. Chop onion and bell pepper and add garlic. Add corn and tomato. Season with cumin, salt, and pepper. This is an easy go-to summer and early fall dish that we eat often, with most of this coming straight out of the garden—especially when grilling some *tado* (meat)!

PASSED DOWN, GENERATION TO GENERATION

Some years ago, Jay pointed out the patch of thorny bushes on the edge of our yard. They grow abundantly at the top of the hillside before the descent into the trees and valley below where Mni Oȟdoka Taŋka flows. He shared, "I used to pick these for my grandma when I was a kid. They're gooseberries." Jay spent much of his childhood at his grandma Valeska and grandpa Willard's farm near Veblen, South Dakota. The farm is part of the Ḣeipa District of the Lake Traverse Reservation. Over the years, he has shared fond memories of his grandma. She doted on "Jay-Jay," and he reciprocated her affection by helping her with small chores. This included gathering *wicahdeśka*—gooseberries. She would make a pie or can jam with the small, dark-purple, burgundy-colored globes. He recalled that she also threw in a few tart green ones. It was such a precious memory he had shared with me that I felt compelled to attempt to elicit this tender remembrance between

Perfectly Balanced Succotash.

grandchild and grandmother. And so, I researched gooseberry pie recipes on the internet and pulled out my mom's trusty pie crust recipe from my collection. I would need only five cups of goose-berries. *Only* five cups. How would I have known how tedious the task would be? Gathering five cups and destemming both ends would take me several hours. But we both remember that first pie. How deliciously tart it was and sweet the memory bridging the past to the present.

After the discovery of the berries, Jay cleared some of the less desirable plants—namely, buckthorn—from the area. As a result, the gooseberries flourished, and we now have a nice patch of them. Each year, around July, we forage *wicahdeśka* from our land. They seem to prefer spaces close to shady areas. Our patch is located on the edge of the lawn, just as you enter the woods and descend the hillside. Their bushes have sharp thorns, like those on roses, to deter us from picking. I try not to fret. They are just trying to make me slow down and take a breath. The darker the berry, the riper and sweeter they are. But just like Jay and his grandma, I pick a few green ones too. I gather as many as I can before I am chased out by the mosquitoes and thorns, leaving some to ripen for the birds. A good once-a-year pie will require more than what I can find some years. On those every-other lean years, I adapt and make a delicious gooseberry sauce to top shortbread.

No one enjoys eating little sticks in their pie and so I will spend a tedious evening removing the stems from both ends. Purpled, juicy fingers cause the stems to stick to my fingertips and cause me to question if the pie is truly worth it. There is likely a can of gooseberries I could buy. I checked—No, there is not! But maybe I could settle for blueberries, I try to convince myself. *Kitaŋh!* Finally, the task is complete. I store the stemless treasures in the fridge as the evening has run out of time.

The next morning, I venture to make a deserving pie crust to hold the delectably tart treasure. I pull the worn index card with my mom's simple pie crust recipe. My mom has always made good bread and pies—just like her mother. I had many previously failed attempts, before I was able to produce a decent crust. It seems maturity helps to make a good pie crust. I believe it comes from having some gray hair coupled with love memories that extend out to my fingertips to knead good pie dough. I also learned it helps to have a pastry mat, dough blender, and a wooden pin clothed in a pastry sock that helps prevent the dough from sticking.

Once I have the two kneaded crusts ready, it is time to transform the stemless beauties into a sticky, semisweet filling. On medium heat, melt a little butter. Then add the berries, a little lemon zest, and some sugar. Not too much—I like my pies tart! Taste as you go along. Simmer until done (my common cooking instruction). Okay, maybe for fifteen minutes for those who dislike ambiguity. If it doesn't thicken, add a little cornstarch in a bit of water. While it is cooling, I put the first crust in a pie pan and baste it with a little whisked egg white as that helps prevent soggy crusts. After the pie filling cools, scoop it onto the bottom pie crust. Cover with the second crust, pinching the edges together. Make some slits in the top crust for ventilation. Baste the top with some egg white wash to give a crispy shine, and sprinkle with a little sugar. Bake at 350 degrees for about an hour. Be sure to let it cool for a while so that the filling sets up a bit. I make some simple whipped cream, sweetened with a little of our maple syrup, and top that baby. I invite special guests to join us for this annual ritual. I choose the kind of relatives or friends who will ooh and ahh with us because they know spending many hours picking off stems is so worth it.

❖   ❖   ❖   ❖

Gooseberry Pie

Mom's Pie Crust
2 cups flour
1 teaspoon salt
⅔ cup shortening
5–7 tablespoons ice water

Combine the ingredients using a dough blender. Divide into two balls. With a clothed pin, roll your dough out into a thin circle onto the pastry mat. This makes two rounds, one for the bottom and top. One trick is to roll the dough around the rolling pin and then unroll it into the pie pan.

Gooseberry Filling
2 teaspoons butter
5 cups berries, minimum (stems removed)
1½ cups sugar
zest from one lemon
corn starch (optional)

In a pot, add butter, berries, and sugar over medium heat. Bring to a simmer, continuing to stir. Add the zest. If it needs thickening, add a little water to cornstarch and blend, continuing to stir.

recipe continued ▶

Whipped Cream
1 pint of real whipping cream
2 tablespoons sugar or maple syrup

Whip cream with a hand mixer until peaks start to form.
Then add sugar or syrup and mix.

AWAKENS THE SENSES

Yesterday I went to bed with joy as we finally received an inch of beautiful, gorgeous rain after days, weeks, really an all-summer drought. I'm lying in bed awake and to my delight, I can hear the rain again. It is very early morning while I listen to the tinkle and ping, light rain falling. It is that time of the morning when the house is still and void of human sounds. So, I do something I never do. I make my way out in pajamas to the edible plant community *before* my body is caffeinated. I step outside and breathe in the earthy odor of rain. My ears fill with the delightful songs of the bird nation, presumably rejoicing from the recent rain. I see the grass is already turning back to green. And I witness the plants perking up before my very eyes. I check the rain gauge, another .25 inch—a small amount, really, but "I'll take it," I say to myself. I decide to pick some kale for a breakfast smoothie. It is my personal remedy for eating too many salty snacks the day before. I gather kale leaves, keeping only those that did not have any of the camouflaged green worms attached. They seem to like munching away on the tasty lacinato kale, more commonly referred to as the dinosaur kale. Nor do I keep the leaves that are speckled with yellow dots. Those are covered in their offspring—eggs that will result in future worms.

While bent over picking, I suddenly hear the rattling chattery noises, the sounds make me feel like I am in a jungle. *DRRRRRR.* I have heard this sound before but never this close. Previously, I wondered if they were birds. I cock my head to the side. I could sense that whatever it was, was just up in the pine trees on the north side of my garden. *DRRRRRRR.* I hear it again and then a higher-pitched *drrrrrr.* This one seemed to be in response, a sort of frantic defensive plea. With kale leaves in hand, I quietly walk toward the sound. Sensing me, they move a little farther away. But again, I hear them. They chatter back and forth. Trying to peer through the maze of branches, I finally catch a glimpse of reddish-brown hair. Oh! They are not birds. I would have seen wings take flight, but nothing. Suddenly, I could see branches moving. *Cinto!* Of course—they are squirrels! Perhaps they are *zica*, red squirrels. The higher-pitched *drrrrrr* sound, I assume, is a younger one. As I continued listening, I sensed it was a mama scolding one of her children. What had happened? Did her young one become too greedy and eat all the breakfast nuts that were intended to feed the whole family? Did they stay out late carousing around and just returned home too tired for morning chores? Did they knock their nest over—do they nest? I need to find out the nature of the noisy family living in the neighborhood.

The DNR website states, "Red squirrels are very vocal." Yeah, no kidding. As I read, I understand why they live here along the long row of conifers lining our property. It provides year-round food for them. Red squirrels make leaf nests in tree cavities or the crotch of a tree. They have two to five babies in the spring, and the kits become independent twelve weeks later. So, that would make these younger ones independent about now.

Maybe her offspring didn't want to leave. "Please, Mama, I don't want to live alone." "It is time to move out, Johnny, time for you to find your own food and make your own nest." She—I'm assuming now it is a momma squirrel—rattles back louder each time the three-month-old pleads. I finish my harvest by picking a few green beans left on plants that are slowly dying off. I munch on one of the crunchy, grassy-tasting beans as my ears prick up for more squirrel conversation. A few yellow leaves drop as my hand brushes up against them. I decided to move indoors. Curious and a bit sad now, I think about my chattery neighbors as I thaw some strawberries to accompany the kale and doctor up my cup of coffee. Their chatter got me missing all my boys, who have left our own nest on the hill.

✦   ✦   ✦   ✦

Triple Berry Smoothie

1 cup strawberries
1 cup blackberries
1 cup raspberries
2 cups chopped kale
1 ripe banana
1 tablespoon chia seeds
4–6 ounces coconut water

Semi-thaw frozen berries. Toss everything in a blender and serve!

RESOURCEFUL AND PATIENT

At least once a week, I will build an entire meal around leftovers or foods that are going to go bad in a short time. Some may say I'm thrifty, but I would call it resourceful. Herbs, too, are so easy to grow and dry for later use. I have grown and dried basil, oregano, thyme, lemon thyme, rosemary, parsley, chives, cilantro, and coriander seed. I also dry paprika and various hot peppers, then grind and jar my own, using recycled spice jars for storage. So many of the decisions and actions I make today are connected to the farming lifestyle I grew up in. I watched my mom cook and bake homemade meals and preserve vegetables from the garden and the hogs and chickens we raised. She threw out very little and made do with what was available, from mending clothes, including worn-out blue jeans, to rinsing and reusing bags and tinfoil. She was and remains resourceful. I also believe this trait comes from Native values rooted in generations of resilience, adaptability, and contentedness.

Yet, resourcefulness also requires ingenuity. It is evident in the hardwood ash used to lye our traditional dried corn for *paśdayapi* (our traditional corn soup). The ingenuity evident in smudging ourselves with prairie sage to purify our body, mind, and spirit. In addition, sage acts as a mosquito repellant and works to eliminate germs and toxins throughout our homes. It is also in the brain-tanned leather once used for shelter and clothing. Using the brain of the animal whose hide is being softened is part of the procedure. It is the same process my dekśi still uses today (except he uses pig brains with deer hides) to make his own buckskin and the hundreds of moccasins he beads. These are the things I am pondering as I sit with a big bowl of blanched cobs of sweet corn on my lap—another long-standing tradition.

It is *Wasutoŋ Wi*, the Moon When the Corn Is Gathered or the Harvest Moon. Every few years in August, I commit to preparing dried corn to make *waskuya*, a soup, just as my *kuŋśi* taught me years ago. I have grown my own sweet corn, only to acquiesce to gathering sweet corn from other growers instead. The *wica* typically would wipe out half my corn the night before harvest. It was as if the raccoons, too, were checking the corn for readiness each evening for days up until harvest. These gardening years were frustrating.

Now, I alternate years of corn planting between our traditional corn and Dakota popcorn. Corn will invariably cross-pollinate, and my garden space is not large enough to accommodate any adequate distance to avoid cross-pollination. It is already a feat to distance my garden from the field corn of nearby neighbors. Speaking of field corn, *kuŋśi* also shared with me that it could be used for making this traditional dried corn. After test tasting a kernel of field corn, I questioned her suggestion. I surmised that those were used during famine as it tasted horrible. Yet long after *Kuŋśi* was gone, I asked another elder from Sisseton about her suggestion. And sure enough, he confirmed that it was done but they would add a little sugar to it. Still, I am grateful that there is plenty of sweet corn available.

After *Kuŋśi*'s hands-on corn-drying lesson, I took on the tradition and would either grow or buy corn from local stands dotting nearby towns and highways in the late summer. One year, a fellow food grower a few miles away offered their leftover sweet corn from their field. I had missed the prime corn that they sell at farmers' markets, but I was welcome to take all the remaining corn I wanted at no charge. The corn was a bit overripe and from the secondary cobs that are often smaller or are only half-filled with kernels. I did not mind. After all, it was free and provided me that sense of resourcefulness, as this corn would have been left to rot. Additionally, just slightly overripe is perfect for the dried corn I was preparing. The sweet corn we all love to slather up with butter and salt during the short seasonal window is best when super-juicy. Perfectly ripe or just underripe is perfect for fulfilling that desire for juice to squirt all over your face as you chomp down on the cob. But trying to dry corn at that stage is a frustrating and futile endeavor. Let me explain and you will understand why.

After husking the corn, you blanch it. This involves placing corn cobs in boiling water for just a minute or two, followed with putting them in ice water to stop the cooking process, and then standing the cobs upright to dry a bit. Because this process is cumbersome, I prefer to do a big batch every few years, which involves several dozen ears. After blanching, I then sit down with a big bowl and begin to individually remove each corn kernel from the cob by hand. My *kuŋśi*'s tips included using a spoon to remove the kernels, but I have never mastered that method. However, I

Shelling corn to dry.

have acquired great control over my thumbs and can use them to remove each kernel unbroken. This keeps the corn germ intact. Amateurs will cut the corn off with a knife, which does not keep the germ connected. The outcome is dried-out corn that resembles a sawdust texture and bland flavor. An intact dried kernel, when added to liquid like soup will puff back up to a juicy kernel and restore that sweet flavor. The process does take quite some time, depending on the cob's ripeness and the amount of corn to dry. For a couple of dozen ears from start to dry, I can typically complete the process in five to six days.

When I get close to finishing a nice bowl full of shelled kernels, I have Jay prepare the screens. We use old window screens that he scrubs and hoses off outside. He sets up sawhorses with boards wide enough to fit four to five screen sets. With each bowlful, I spread the kernels on the screens and cover them with another, ensuring there are no gaps for flies and moths to go through. Then we let the sun do her magic in drying the corn. Invariably, during this multi-day process in August, it will rain or there will be a humid day here and there. On those days, I will bring the screens indoors and put them in front of a fan until I can resume the sun-drying process. You might be wondering by now why I don't just use a dehydrator. Trust me. There is something about sun-dried corn that has a much better flavor. There is a reason the process with time-consuming traditions remains steadfast.

✦   ✦   ✦   ✦

Waskuya

2–3 pounds meat (venison, beef, or bison roast or steaks)
1–2 cups dried sweet corn
2 large potatoes (optional)
2 onions
water to fill the pot
seasoning to taste

Cube the meat and add to a big soup pot. Add water to cover and begin cooking. Pour in desired amount of stored dried corn. Cube potatoes and add. Chop onions and add. Season to taste. Fill with more water. Cook for several hours.

Ptaŋyetu

UNTO THEE

I tromp Indigenous and man-made heel to toe
Repeatedly
Over the cracked and worn, now uncovered.
With metal and fire, I rake and burn.
I move and dig, steel turning, sometimes hitting rock
Repeatedly
Through it until malleable, now revealed.
I furrow and stab, creating gullies and holes
Poking them full of grit and faith, and births consecrated
    with prayers
Repeatedly
Now thirsty for rays and drips and drops.
With tender soles and soft-handed strokes
I tip and toe, pause and pat
Repeatedly
Over the lush and living, now covered.
With flesh and hide, I sway and jig
Twirling and swaying
Repeatedly
Dancing unto thee.

Fall
The Time of the Otter

▲▲▲

DRAWS ON THE WISDOM OF PROTOCOL

I am staring at several bushels of pears grouped on our kitchen floor, questioning whether I need to sort them. I could just hand out random sizes to the willing pear takers. Yet, the voice in the back of my mind directs me otherwise. I begin to gather several bags and boxes while Jay brings me the heavy containers of pears. I plop down on the floor and sit crossed-legged, amongst bags, boxes, and oodles of pears, and begin to sort. I look over each pear and then decide if it goes in the box for canning, in bags for pear-loving friends and family, or in a small bushel basket for drying.

Here is how I make the decision for each pear: If they are larger in size with no blemishes or perhaps one small imperfection, they go in the canning box to continue ripening. That's right. We pick the pears from the tree before they are fully ripe. Pears are brought indoors and when stored together emit ethylene, a gas that causes them to ripen (think of bananas). As I continue my sorting, I place small-to-medium-size pears with no blemishes into gift bags. These I will deliver to various places—our Indian church, the tribal offices, the local public television station, Dakota Wicoḣaŋ, Uncle's house, and a couple of friends' homes. Pears that have less than desirable flaws like obvious bug festering, I place in a basket off to the side. These too will sit to ripen.

As they do, I peel them, and cut into slices about one-quarter-inch thick, discarding the bad parts, and plop them in lemon water. Once I have enough to dry, I strain them and situate the slices onto the dehydrator screens and slide the screens back into the shelves. It takes four to six hours for each batch to dry adequately. I then store the dehydrated pears in a cute wire-flip-top jar on the counter. They are so deliciously sweet and are enjoyed throughout the year. *Ptaŋyetu,* the Time of the Otter, marks the beginning of the great harvest. And while our family shares in the work and the fruits of our collective labor, there is always more than we can eat and store.

This year, the chore of preserving the pears was mine alone because Mom was not feeling up to canning post surgery. They are an incredible amount of work, but my dad just loves pears, and the taste of our homegrown pears is unmatched. We usually can pears in quart jars, but this year I canned half the pears in wide-mouth pints and the other half in the traditional wide-mouth quarts. While perhaps less efficient, the pints are more easily eaten up in a couple of days, whereas, once opened, the quarts tend to sit in the refrigerator longer. I decide then that moving forward, this will be a new tradition amongst the many pear protocols we practice.

Now that the pear preserving is under way, I start thinking about this year's apples. They continued to drop off the trees this year, long past the standard "June drop," I suspect because of the lack of moisture. The tree in its wisdom is dropping its fruit to conserve energy and save itself. Jay has been cleaning them up by the wheelbarrowful. Occasionally, I will pick one up off the ground that looks decent and take a bite. They are delicious despite their small size. With each passing day, my concern increases that there won't be any apples left to make cider. Then just today, to my surprise, I walked into the kitchen and there sat a basket full of Honey Crisp apples. These Jay had gathered up from the ground and instead of throwing them into the wheelbarrow to toss, he brought them inside. "Maybe you can dry these too," he said. We have been together so long that he knew how happy it made me to make use of the apples wasting on the ground and that despite the tree having had to drop them due to lack of moisture, they would be appreciated.

✦ ✦ ✦ ✦

Pear Muffins

2 cups flour
2 teaspoon baking powder
½ teaspoon salt
2 teaspoons cinnamon
½ cup brown sugar
1 egg
¼ cup oil
⅔ cup milk
2 cups diced pears

Combine dry ingredients well. Mix egg, oil, and milk together, then add to dry ingredients. Fold in diced pears. I freeze chopped pears each year, putting 2 heaping cups of chopped pear in each bag. If using thawed frozen pears, drain some, not all, of the excess water before adding. Scoop batter into greased muffin tins. Bake at 350 for 20 minutes. Check with a toothpick: if there is still dough on the toothpick when inserted, it needs more time in the oven.

ATTRACTS GRATITUDE

Slightly amused, I gently grab the tiny ant between my thumb and finger and remove it from the piece of oat granola it appears to be hiding underneath. I drop the small brown harmless insect to the ground and know I have likely eaten at least one of its relatives this morning. I continue to enjoy how the sweet and tart beads of blackberries pop in my mouth. They are coupled with the smoky sweetness of last year's maple syrup harvest swirled in the plain unsweetened yogurt. It makes for a seasonal treat. I'm enjoying the meal this early fall Sunday morning, still in pajamas while sitting on the east-facing front porch.

With squinting eyes, I am relishing the colors of the rising sun contrasted against the prairie setting. The sun is slightly above the dark bluff on the other side of the vast river valley, folded into a layer above of light blue sky. Shades of dark greens fill the faraway landscape. As my gaze closes in, hues of prairie gold appear. My head turns from side to side, taking in our front hillside with nine towering Autumn Blaze maple trees. I notice their tops are just starting to turn the burgundy color they are named for. These are the same maples that enhance my morning breakfast, and the ones Jay taps each year.

I take in a deep breath of air and its crisp earthy smell reminds me of the change happening. I rub my upper arms in an attempt to create heat. It is a bit chilly out, jacket weather really. But I am wanting to soak in the vitamin D that we will soon need to take from a bottle. This morning's trip to the garden garnered over a cup of delicious berries. The thorny patch is still producing well into the fall. While we are experiencing climate change more than ever, the extended growing season brings an abundance of fruit. Last year's harvest was cut short with an early morning frost while the bushes were still loaded with unripen berries.

Sunrise from the front deck.

My attention is drawn to two crickets chirping out of sync. I hear an occasional car drive by—I assume they are heading to town, perhaps to church. I decided not to feel guilty today as it's been some time since I last went to our little church on the rez. "Soon," I tell myself—I miss the *Dakota dowaŋpi* (singing) and the few friends and family that attend. But for today, I'll rejoice in this beautiful early autumn day. *Wakaŋ Taŋka Tuŋkaŋśida, de aŋpetu teca aŋpetu waśte heoŋ wopida epe!* Creator-Grandfather, today is a new day and therefore I say thank you!

ABUNDANCE

Our growing seasons seem to be longer and the weather more erratic. Certainly, the climate is changing, and a lot is at stake. Hot dry spells and drought have taken a toll on lands across the country. Yet, I am amazed at the resilience of our plant relatives. While many wilted during the hotter than normal temperatures, some seemed to flourish. One year, the twenty tomato plants I seeded and transplanted in the garden were prolific. Their thick stems provided the stability for the plants to grow and tower above my head. I carefully maneuvered through the tomato jungle gathering more tomatoes than I knew what to do with. We were well into October, and I saw another round of blossoms coming again from the indeterminate varieties. Determinates stop growing and producing at a particular plant height and do not require staking. Indeterminates continue to grow and pro- duce an indefinite amount. And that they did. They continued throughout the unusually long season. My plan this particular year was to double the canning so as not have to plant tomatoes the following year. It worked! We continued to nosh on canned pints of tomato soup, salsa, and quarts of spaghetti sauce the following year. Frozen quart bags of tomatoes and tomato sauce filled the freezer. We preserved an abundance from that drawn- out tomato harvest. Not to mention that I ate an unprecedented number of BLTs that held thick slices of Hungarian hearts. I also made batches of bruschetta for Walker, my youngest son, and me to devour. And I made fresh tomato bisque and several other recipes with fresh tomatoes. I literally ate so many Federles, Hungarian hearts, Amish pastes, and Cherokee Purples that I had canker sores in my mouth for a good month. I needed to move out of the oohing, aahing, and drooling stage every gardener finds themselves at during tomato season. I needed to transition from my own too-much-acid phase to seek out opportunities to relive the oohing and aahing via someone else. So, I started making special deliveries to family and friends—tomato giveaways, if you will. I would boast about the flavors of the heirloom tomatoes and the meatiness of my favorites. "You'll love them, they aren't all water and seeds," I said convincingly to those who agreed to take some. Sometimes I did, in fact, get a call or text later about how delicious they were. I enthusiastically agreed when my longtime friend Mary reported, "Still eating tomato sandwiches twice a day. They'll be a happy memory this winter." I decided not to warn my curly-haired Irish friend of the acid breakout she was sure to get but instead offered up more tomatoes. To my great satisfaction, she'd asked, "Would Tuesday be okay to come over for more tomatoes?" She wanted to bring her grandson, hoping to relive her own tomato delight through him.

Next, I visited my uncle Super. His real name is Walter, but everyone knows him by his childhood nickname "Super," which is its own story. Dressed in a T-shirt and blue jeans, Uncle was sitting in his usual spot. He was camped in the sun porch beading another pair of moccasins. I saw a random tomato on a box behind him, among cowboy hats and containers of dried Indian corn. Each year, I seed enough tomatoes to gift plants to my dad and uncle. So, with flat doubt in my voice, I asked him if he would want any tomatoes. Actually, what I said was, "Dekśi, you probably don't want any more tomatoes, do you?" And to my surprise he said, "Yes, more tomatoes and pears." Unfortunately, I was all out of pears, as I had traded the remaining boxes and boxes of pears with another good friend, Mary Jo. She and I had made a trade agreement for giant tribal heirloom watermelons and squashes

Abundance of tomatoes from the garden.

for my pears. Earlier in the season, I had attempted to save my *wamnu* plants from squash borers. I performed an operation on the stems by removing the squash killers and their babies. Unfortunately, this effort only garnered one squash worth keeping. So, I was beyond excitement to make a produce swap. "Good trade," I had said jokingly and gestured the universal sign for "it's all good and we're square" during the exchange. So that day, even though I wouldn't be able to provide any pears, I was eager to return to the tomato jungle and look for the red nuggets so that Dekši, too, could continue to enjoy tomato delight.

✦   ✦   ✦   ✦

Bruschetta for One

1 medium tomato
half of a small red onion
2 garlic cloves, finely chopped
fresh or dried basil
1–2 tablespoons olive oil
1 tablespoon balsamic vinegar
salt and pepper

Chop tomato and red onion and add to bowl. Add garlic cloves. Chop fresh basil or crush dried basil and add to bowl, along with olive oil and balsamic vinegar. Season with salt and pepper to taste. Let sit for 5 minutes while you toast garlic cheese toast. Liberally top the bread with tomato mix with each bite. This is addictive enough to eat every day for lunch until the tomato season is over.

✦   ✦   ✦   ✦

Spaghetti Sauce, canned

12 quarts quartered and peeled tomatoes
3 cups chopped onions
3 cups chopped green peppers
1 bulb garlic
2 tablespoons dried basil
$\frac{1}{8}$ cup canning salt
1 tablespoon pepper
$\frac{1}{2}$ cup sugar

Blanch tomatoes so that you can peel skins (blanching involves immersing in boiling water for a minute or two and then in ice-cold water). Loosely chop tomatoes in quarters or smaller (depending on how chunky you like spaghetti sauce, but tomatoes will cook down smaller too). Add to a 16-quart pot. Add remaining ingredients. Bring to a boil and reduce to a simmer. Cook down to desired consistency. Fill sterilized quart jars, leaving $\frac{1}{2}$-inch headspace. Add a couple of drops of commercially bottled lemon juice. Process for 35 minutes in hot water bath.

A SHARED EXPERIENCE

All Natives love their soup. Well, Dakotas anyway, or shall I say, *most* Dakotas. This belief of mine is why I challenge my youngest son's soup sentiment: "Meh, I don't really like soup." "What kind of Indian are you?" I asked him. We have this conversation often because, well, I make a lot of soup, especially bean soup. I read once that there are more than four hundred varieties of beans. Perhaps many of those are now stored in vaults, but I imagine Indigenous people all over Turtle Island have at least one bean soup recipe they have relied on for time immemorial.

I am craving my go-to bean soup, despite the fact that we are still finishing up another pot of soup. This time, I chose the Hidatsa White Shield beans—*Ama'ca ita' wina' ki matu'hica* ("shield-figured bean" in the Hidatsa language). This pole bean is not as prolific as other bean varieties I grow, but it remains a favorite. It is one of those hearty bean soup varieties that pairs well with ham bone. I don't recall now how I acquired this seed, perhaps from a fellow heirloom gardener or I ordered it from Seed Savers. Regardless, I have maintained its seed stock by replanting year after year. I read that the Hidatsa White Shield bean's Latin name is *Phaseolus vulgaris.* I wondered how an heirloom, originally grown on the Missouri River by the Hidatsa people, acquired a Latin name. But then I learned that all pole and bush beans are bestowed with this foreign name. After a little more research, I further learned that the Roman-based language is used to scientifically name all plants so as to maintain a common language across peoples. The Hidatsa White Shield, or rather *Phaseolus vulgaris,* or the "common bean," is anything but common. The plump, large, egg-shaped bean has a tan circle with maroonish-brown markings that somewhat resemble a shield. The Hidatsa White Shield is just one of many beans, yet it certainly is not found in the grocery store. I have only seen spotted pinto, navy, and black beans among the inexpensive bags of legumes. Common canned beans—kidney, butter, garbanzo, and great northern seem generic to me. It is as if the beans became monocultured, their uniqueness washed away, their stories forgotten. Not once have I seen the beautiful heir-loom varieties in stores that are found displayed on my kitchen counter—Mandan Black, Hidatsa Red, Hopi Black Turtle, Bumble Bee, Tiger's Eye, Good Mother Stallard, Christmas Lima, Scarlet Runner, Tohono O'odham Brown and White Tepary, Painted Pony, Arikara Yellow, Cherokee Red Peanut, Lina Sisco's Bird Egg, and of course the Hidatsa White Shield. Each one is unique in color and shape, boiling time, flavor, and ideal preparation style. And of course, we know the health and nutritional benefits of beans. They are considered a slow-release food, thus ideal for diabetics. They are also high in protein and fiber. I have substituted them for meat, although my carnivore partner really prefers meat in every meal. One health trick I adopted when making tacos was by incor-porating approximately half beans to cut down on the red meat that dietitians now tell us to eat in moderation. Beans also have a good list of vitamins (e.g., folate, thiamine) and minerals (e.g., iron, magnesium) with potential health benefits ranging from reduced cholesterol to lower blood sugar.

Beans are so easy to grow. I learned to change up the variety of beans I plant each year as I would have no room for anything else if I planted all the varieties I have now acquired. I also like to plant beans through the three sisters (corn, beans, squash) method. Planting them together creates symbiosis, sort of like mutual aid. Beans provide a source of nitrogen while corn requires a lot of it to grow. In turn, the corn provides something for vining beans to grow on; and the squash leaves temper weeds and help retain moisture surrounding the other plants. While I have not yet tried planting the Hidatsa White Shield next to my corn, as Buffalo Bird Woman details, I have planted half runners and even bush beans at the base of the corn stalks. I usually plant the pole beans along a fence that I move around each year or alternate with peas. This past season, I planted more Hidatsa White Shield seed than usual because it is one of the beans I use up each year. I also do not tread my beans as she describes but rather sit with a couple of big bowls and shell by hand while watching television. Buf-falo Bird Woman would think I was crazy. She shared this story,

Hopi Black Turtle beans.

as related by Gilbert Livingstone Wilson in *Buffalo Bird Woman's Garden* (1987):

> White men do not seem to know very much about raising
> beans. Our school teacher last year raised beans in a field
> near the school-house; and when harvest time came, he tried
> to pluck the pods directly into a basket, without treading or
> threshing the vines. I think it would take him a very long time
> to harvest his beans in that manner. (85)

I grow and store maybe ten quarts of beans each year, certainly
not the three barrels Buffalo Bird Woman prepared that served
as a protein staple for her people each year. Perhaps next year I
will try treading and threshing like she did just to gain the experience. After the bean vines and bushes were fully dry, instead
of shelling them by hand, I could heap them onto a borrowed
tarp of Jay's perhaps. Then, I could put on a pair of my moccasins
and trample over the vines, thus releasing the beans. Buffalo Bird

Woman describes using a stick to beat any remaining beans lose from pods that hadn't been freed. After removing the dried vines, I would continue the winnowing, like I do today. I gently toss the beans in a colander (versus a wooden bowl) on a windy day which helps to remove any debris and remaining bean particles. I can understand why she thought hand shelling a ridiculous practice, especially for a large harvest. Maybe I would need to sow my entire garden in beans and see if I can't harvest barrels full. Certainly, I wouldn't need to plant beans for several years. But then again, I would miss my tomatoes, corn, peppers, garlic . . . and of course the joy in gathering and shelling bean pods by hand each fall.

Eyeballing it, I pour the big white beans from the pretty ocean-colored antique jar into a bowl. I will cover them with water to soak overnight, which will start to soften them. There really hasn't been a time I made too many beans as Jay has been known to eat five bowls in one sitting. We are both grateful that we don't share a bathroom but acknowledge that *wahaŋpi* (soup) is best shared together.

✦   ✦   ✦   ✦

Omnica Wahaŋpi

2 cups dried beans
1–2 tablespoons oil
3–4 stalks celery, chopped
1 onion, chopped
2 garlic cloves, chopped
1 cup finely chopped carrots
chicken broth or water
1–2 bay leaves
ham bone or 2 cups of chopped ham
salt and pepper
2 slices bacon cooked and chopped (optional)

Soak beans overnight (options: Hidatsa White Shield, Bumble Bee, Carolina Contender, Arikara Yellow, Lina Sisco's Bird Egg, or similar). Strain and rinse beans when ready to make soup. To reduce cooking time, cook beans in water before making soup. In large soup pot (I prefer my enameled cast iron pot), add oil and heat on medium heat. Add celery and onion, cook about 5 minutes until tender. Add garlic, stir, and cook for one more minute. Add remaining ingredients. Cover pot and bring to a boil. Then turn heat down to a simmer and cook for 2–3 hours until beans are soft. Eat no more than five bowls.

Omnica Wahaŋpi.

OPEN TO ANYONE AND EVERYONE

I have had many visitors to our gardens. Sometimes people are interested in starting their own garden or just want tips. Other times they are fellow gardeners who just want to talk garden and perhaps share produce. I have had college students and professors visit my garden. Even Mary Holm and her film crew from *Prairie Yard and Garden* have come out. I have taken lots of friends and family out to the garden, too; some were eager and willing, others I have dragged. But I think my favorite garden guests are children. Most of the kids who have visited have had limited or no exposure to gardens, foraging, and food production. The questions, curiosity, and engagement from those growing minds encourage me. They often do not know where the everyday food we eat comes from, nor have they tasted fresh produce. Yet, they are the most entertaining visitors. I think the most telling question I had was, "Where is the salsa tree?" The other day, I had a few of these fun garden tourists drop by. My tomato-loving friend Mary brought out three of her grandchildren, Dante, Ameyrah, and Madden. While usually we would have put the garden to bed by then, the weird lingering warm weather brought about a resurgence—a second crop of sorts from spent plants. I had decided to leave the spent plants in the ground this year instead of clearing the beds for winter. I did this as I understand the practice provides sustenance for the microbes in the ground. Well, since we had not had a frost yet, the leftover plants started reproducing, along with those plants that were lingering through the extended season—like kale, blackberries, and tomatoes. So, the three kids and I foraged for the reproducing garden goodies.

Madden, the youngest, perhaps six or seven years old, flitted from plant to plant, jabbering and asking questions nonstop. He reminded me of a bee moving from blossom to blossom seeking nectar, except he was looking for remnant edibles. Together, we found and gathered tiny Dakota popcorn cobs, salad greens, peppers, and kale leaves. Mary, along with Ameyrah, who was about the same age as Madden, wanted flower bouquets. So, we picked zinnias and marigolds for several arrangements. We then moved over to the blackberries that were still producing. Dante, a preteen and more reposed than young Madden, yet still inquisitive, found a nearly ripened blackberry. He asked if he could eat it. I said, "Sure, it might be"—he popped it in his mouth before I could finish my sentence—"a little sour yet because of some of that remaining red." To my surprise, he replied, "Mmm." So, I found another one, this time fully ripe, and said, "Try this one, it'll be sweeter." Those are magical moments for me. Seeing the expressions from new experiences on their faces—whether it is a scrunched-up face indicating dislike or the surprised delight in their eyes. That day, Mary's grandkids, like most young visitors, left us adults for other

Zinnias in the garden. Photograph by Tanner Peterson.

ventures—playing with our kitties, walking the hiking trails, and lying in the backyard hammocks. Meanwhile, Mary and I continued the garden foraging and found adult delight in the small handful of raspberries that had restarted post-season—wow, are they confused! We left the garden, Mary with her arms full of second-harvest gifts and I in puzzled wonderment—are those stalks in their first year or is the regrowth considered their second year and meant for cutting back?

✦　　✦　　✦　　✦

Salsa for Canning
20 cups peeled and chopped tomatoes
2 cups chopped green peppers
3 cups chopped onions
2½ tablespoons canning salt
½ cup apple cider vinegar
1–2 cups hot peppers
24 ounces tomato paste
1 tablespoon dried oregano
⅓ cup sugar
1 tablespoon minced garlic

recipe continued ▶

Blanch tomatoes so that you can peel skins. I have also put single-layered tomatoes under the broiler for a couple of minutes (watch closely) to peel skins. Chop tomatoes, peppers, onions. If you like spicy salsa, include seeds and ribs of peppers. Add all ingredients in a nonstick pot(s) and cook for one hour. This recipe is modified from the *Cooking on the Right Track Cookbook* (1999).

To process, fill hot sterilized pints with salsa (I will also do a batch with quart jars that I use in making chili), leaving ½ inch headspace. Add a couple of drops of commercially bottled lemon juice to ensure adequate acidity levels (required for hot water bath). Be sure to wipe down the rims of jars. Process for 15 minutes. The *Ball Blue Book Guide to Preserving* has all the information you need to process just about anything.

Salsa making.

As I headed into town the other day, I passed a field where they were preparing to tile. The field was filled with black plastic tubes snaking across the land, adding to the already fifty-six million acres of tiled fields across the United States, according to the 2017 Census of Agriculture report published by the U.S. Department of Agriculture, National Agricultural Statistics Service. I wondered if the significant amount of drain tiling impacts our planet's fresh water, a mere .03 percent of which is sourced from wetlands. When water is drained from land and then directed to drainage ditches, where does that water eventually end up? I decided to do a little research.

Tiling is a farming practice to convey subsurface water out of the land and into a drainage ditch by burying tubing underground about three to five feet deep. The plastic tubing has little holes throughout to pull water through. The practice is used to dry out wetlands or areas of periodic flooding. Drain tiling is nothing new, and there are early accounts of the process using clay tiles from the Egyptians and Babylonians. Our house and other homes built during and after the 1950s typically have drain tiling around the perimeter, and I am grateful to not have a wet basement in the spring. Yet, in a congressional report, *Wetlands Losses in the United States 1780s to 1980s,* from the U.S. Department of Interior's Fish and Wildlife Service, I learned draining wetlands across the Midwest began in earnest in the early 1900s in support of expanding agriculture. In the 1980s, the wetlands conservation movement caused a momentary decrease in tiling practices. Yet a couple of decades later, increased land and crop prices spurred a resurgence in tiling. According to some sources, tiling can provide a 15–25 percent increase in crop yields. Gaining early access to fields in the spring and not having to return to sections once they dry out, for example, contributes to saving time and boosting yields. More recently, according to the Agriculture Drainage Management Coalition, there are new efforts in creative modifications to temper the speed and amount of drainage by changing the height of the water outlet.

I'll admit I don't know the engineering and calculations of tiling, but this field seemed like overkill and I wondered if the expense was worth it. After commenting about this to Jay, he shared that he had seen an old photograph earlier of a local lake in what appeared to be the same location. He said the caption read "Lake Belview." Really! There was a Lake Belview? I wondered where the lake had gone. Is it possible that their efforts were literally tiling out the remnants of a lake? Likely it was a small lake—and perhaps it was more of a prairie pothole that gained lake status during a wet year.

After doing a little more digging, I pulled up a local drainage story gone political. In the county next over, a drainage ditch project was approved by county commissioners that would allow subsurface water to drain into Limbo Creek. The Minnesota Department of Natural Resources got involved and declared that Limbo Creek was a protected waterway and the project would require an environmental review. The issue ended up at the state's supreme court. Here's the backstory: During the 1980s, Minnesota's Public Waters Inventory erroneously listed Limbo Creek as a "public ditch," leaving it vulnerable to channeling. In 2017, the Minnesota Department of Natural Resources removed Limbo Creek from their inventory, further leaving it with no protection, because even public ditches require permits for modification. Limbo Creek is the only natural remaining waterway in Renville County. According to the Minnesota Center for Environmental Advocacy, Renville County is now 90 percent drained, with more drainage ditches than roads. Can that be true? I pull up Google Earth and search for Limbo Creek, which snakes and eventually drains into the Minnesota River. I scan out to follow the creek away from the river and notice that the creek straightens, often following field lines and boundaries. How can that be?

Drain tiling, channeling, and straightening natural waterways like creeks and streams maximize acreage. Yet, eliminating the natural hydrology environment—the curves, the prairie potholes, the prairie vegetation near waterways—moves water much more quickly. Why should any of this matter? The rain that falls in Renville County and part of the drain tiling system enters the Wakpamnisota within forty-eight hours, along with sediments and fertilizer (nitrogen and phosphorus). And without the wetlands, the water doesn't get filtered and cleaned along the way; thus the excess nitrogen and phosphorus create algae blooms, ultimately suffocating life. To top it off, soil erosion increases owing to swift-moving waters. It impacts everyone along the river all the way down to the Gulf of Mexico.

There are people supporting water and environmental rights, including the Minnesota Center for Environmental Advocacy and

Voices Driving Change, who are protecting wetlands from farm drainage systems. And there are people, *ikce wicaśta*—common people—who are advocating and speaking up for clean water. For now, it has been decided that an environmental review will need to be done before a decision will be made about the future of Limbo Creek.

Recently, I was huddled in conversation about land with a diverse group of folks at a local fundraiser. A farmer piqued my interest when he spoke about drain tiling. I leaned forward and worked hard to suspend my judgments and seek understanding of the why. Why do we continue to whittle away the remaining wetlands and prairie potholes in between the vast acres of corn and bean fields? I listened as he explained how one of his acres had been too wet to produce much. And in a prior year, the flooding caused the crop to fail, thus bringing in no money from that acre of land. So, he made the decision to drain-tile that area, at a cost of seven hundred dollars. He proudly shared that the following year, that same acre produced forty bushels of corn. He estimated corn valued at five dollars per bushel, bringing the value up in one year by two hundred dollars. The return on investment (there's that measuring stick again) would be within four to five years. He continued to share the benefits of laying the black plastic tubing. It draws moisture away—allowing earlier tilling and planting for optimal yields and fewer problems if there were wet conditions at harvest. He later exclaimed that any banker would grant a loan on that kind of improvement. But is it an improvement? Perhaps a short-term monetary gain, but at what long-term cost? I believe we ought to consider water quality, land and animal stewardship, and care of our relatives downstream as well. As with many of these types of conversations, I was disappointed to hear that it comes down to economics. Whether we are talking literally about money, or some other metric rooted in financial gain or loss and return on investments and time, our society seems to be fixated on analyzing or measuring success based on economics.

My curiosity waned and I made note once again of my perceived differences between mainstream and Native worldviews.

While I try not to generalize, I believe Native worldviews prioritize relationships over economics. Profoundly simple and yet deeply complex, *mitakuye owasiŋ*, all my relations, extends far beyond the human family. It extends to the *wamakaśkaŋ oyate* (the animal nation), like the ducks seeking marshy areas and the pollinators wintering in the hollows of long grasses and leaf clutter. It includes the *wato oyate* (plant nation), like the cottonwoods and elms dotting our river valley and the cattails found in wetlands that hold the nests of red-winged blackbirds. Relationships also extend to the wind that carries our ancestors' whispers, the water held within our very cells, and to Mother Earth beneath our feet. How can we help every child, future food producer, prospective teacher, and aspiring legislator to grasp, feel, and understand that we are all related, connected, and interdependent? The connections are felt yet hidden in our daily living while we without regard experience all the many positive benefits of these relatives. How can we ultimately begin to make decisions in a way that is measured by the relational impact instead of our bank accounts?

The notches on our relationship ruler include seven notches on each side of the present moment. This is based on our Dakota view of seven generations past and seven generations of the future. Our decision-making would then assume responsibility. Let's count them: We have a responsibility to our great-great-great-great-great-grandchildren by considering the wisdom and teachings past from our great-great-great-great-great-grandparents. Even when I limit the extension of that relational measuring stick to just me and family, I can still feel the significance. And so, what if we replaced profit and money as the rationale for draining wetlands with a relationality lens instead?

Wetlands like our prairie potholes are depressions left over from the glaciers that scraped across the landscape. They are found all throughout the Midwest, which, according to the Environmental Protection Agency, serves as the world's most important wetlands region. Yet, prairie potholes are disappearing. My friend Patrick, a longtime environmental activist, educated me about the importance of wetlands and prairie potholes. Of Irish descent, he described that at one point "One could literally canoe across this area. Bird Island is named that for a reason yet, no longer apparent." My eyes bugged out a bit as I tried to imagine oodles of potholes, wildlife, and canoes rather than vast fields of corn and beans and the "tractors" that trek across fields, now wider than a road lane and no longer resembling the tractors I drove as a kid. I remember, though, that there is a great view of a collection of remaining potholes on Highway 23 heading south out of Granite Falls. During wet and rainy seasons, one can see them fill up more than other years, resulting in increased marshy plants. Prairie potholes fill up with snowfall and rainwater with some being temporary and others permanent. They serve several important roles. Of course, ducks and geese love these areas and we too love hearing them honk as their V-shaped communities pass overhead. During my childhood, they were regular dinner guests. But I wonder what the benefits of having ducks and geese are beyond sight, sound, and taste. According to Ducks Unlimited, they serve an important role! As waterfowl move from pond to pond, they increase the biodiversity of other species, including frogs, invertebrates, and plants. They hitch rides on the webbed feet of our winged relatives. And the more waterholes we have, the greater the diversity of gene pools. Increased gene pools are critical when facing adversity, like the current climate changes we are experiencing. Ducks and geese also help keep invasive species and insect populations down as part of their diet.

Prairie potholes also help recharge groundwater supplies by temporarily storing water that slowly passes through the ground. These areas capture and filter out excess nitrogen left from agricultural practices. Because these important waterholes store excess water, they then reduce downstream flooding, including overflow to roads and fields. While annual flooding is caused by additional factors beyond draining prairie potholes, according to the Federal Emergency Management Agency the annual cost due to flooding is $17 billion! This cost we all have to pay, and some of those affected by floods endure a larger burden.

I recall some time ago our tribal leadership worked with the

Army Corps of Engineers and perhaps the Environmental Protection Agency. They were working to restore the natural flow and curves in the Wakpamnisota that snakes through our remaining reservation lands. Patrick, a fellow gardening pal and former director of Clean Up the River Environment (CURE) is a big advocate for the environment. He shared that his early environmental fascination began on the prairie while a student at the University of Minnesota, Morris, a small liberal arts college, and another connection we share. I imagine he had some not-so-friendly conversations with these agencies. He recounted a story of meeting one such employee from the Army Corps of Engineers, who handed Patrick his business card and said, "I'm basically here to undo what we've done." Listening to that story, I could see the potential and hope across peoples, lands, and even federal agencies. He shared the frustration he felt over the shortsightedness in some of the environmental decisions. Yet, he described how his advocacy strategies changed by hosting and connecting listening sessions between seemingly opposing parties. He described how each "side" truly believed they were making the right decision. Some headway would be gained by bringing the two opposing sides together to uncover the overlapping intersection (like a Venn diagram) through intentional listening. That sure seems simple enough!

While it does not appear that prairie potholes have any protection, there is some hopeful discussion underway about their future as people begin to understand that there is a connection to larger downstream waterways. When prairie potholes are drained of the excess water from agricultural lands, the benefit of the slow filtering process of nitrogen and phosphorous is lost. Instead, they are carried through these makeshift waterways that eventually end up in our rivers and lakes. Excess nitrogen and phosphorous slowly smother fish and other aquatic life.

Our family loves fishing. Each year, we catch our share of bass, pike, panfish, and a few walleyes. I am quite sure I would miss the time spent with reel in hand sitting in my dad's boat or on the dock, and family fish fries if fishing was no longer viable. Perhaps

Dad, my brother, Rob, and me *(at left)* in 1981.

I would adjust, holding only to those memories. Yet, what none of us can adjust to is a lack of clean water. *Mni wiconi*—water is life, for you, for me, and for the babies we carry in our water wombs. Perhaps it is hard for us to think through these ecosystem connections that lead right back to us. But if we could just imagine. *It's a Wonderful Life* is a favorite movie of mine and I watch it every year. Let's swap George for prairie potholes for a moment and imagine how we would long to wake from a dream that had measured life only through money. Perhaps we would rejoice in the understanding that a rich life is one found in relationships, including our feathered kin, frogs, invertebrates, friends downriver, and you and me.

✦   ✦   ✦   ✦

Fish Fry

2 cups flour
1 tablespoon salt
1½ teaspoon garlic powder
1 teaspoon onion powder

recipe continued ▶

1 teaspoon dried oregano
½ teaspoon pepper
1 teaspoon paprika
¼ teaspoon thyme
¼ teaspoon allspice
1 can of beer
fresh or thawed fish fillets
oil for frying

Pat fish fillets dry and lay out on a cookie sheet. Heat about
2 inches of corn or vegetable oil in a frying pan. Mix dry ingredients together, whisk beer in, enough to make a coating batter.
When oil is hot enough, coat fillets in batter and gently place in
hot oil. Cook for two to three minutes on each side. Then place
the cooked fillets on newspaper and salt. Eat while hot and crispy.
Fish can be eaten without tartar sauce but is best eaten with
homemade dipping sauce. I make ours with real mayonnaise,
finely minced pickles, a dab of pickle juice, and a lot of pepper.
Our family likes to eat fish with handmade French fries but will
accept hand-cut, baked potato wedges and even acquiesce to
store-bought tater tots. Regardless, a potato of sorts helps move
accidental fish bones stuck in throats due to impatient hungry
fish lovers.

PLANNING AND PREPARATION

When the leaves begin to fall, the best seeds are reserved for the
next iteration. Seed saving in and of itself is a deliberate act in
sustainability, sovereignty, and regeneration. I contemplate what
our ancestors would have thought about seed saving. I am cer-
tain it was part of a deliberate practice at the end of each growing
season. Preserving seeds for next year's food source would have
been of upmost concern to ensure future sustenance. Seed swapping with other families, bands, and tribes would also have been
a likely tradition, much like many of us do today. Yet, the motivation between then and now is likely different. Theirs would
have been tied to sustaining life—the lives of their families, children, and grandchildren. Mine, ours is about reclaiming a way

of life. All that has happened in between these generations, the deliberate acts of genocide and colonization, were countered by small deliberate acts that our ancestors took in preserving the varieties of traditional and heirloom seeds. I do not know all of the family and community stories of how the *wamnaheza* seeds were passed from one generation to the next beyond my great-grandpa Wanbdiska and Elsie Cavender—community elders from long ago. Yet, I am grateful to my *dekśi* who taught me, and to all those whose hands shelled, stored, and passed on our corn seed to the next generation. Understanding the deliberate act of saving seeds across generations is reason alone to save and continue to plant our precious seeds.

Saving seeds from various crops each year saves money from not having to purchase them year after year. It is also a reduction in the carbon footprint from ordering, packaging, and shipping seeds. There is a lot of discussion about genetically modified, hybrid, and pretreated seeds, and why farmers may purchase seed every year rather than save seed, for example, corn and soybean stock, for the following year. Some of the benefits discussed are that it saves money from not having to cultivate as much, being able to irrigate less, or reduce insecticide use as these seeds have been engineered or treated accordingly. Yet, I will say that I have found heirloom fruits and vegetables superior in taste and there is something to say about retaining original foods as Creator intended. As I continue to save seeds each year, they adjust to our geography, soil, and climate conditions. I do not remember when I started saving my seeds, but I continue to learn about the process. While I do not save seeds from everything I grow yet, like tomatoes, I do save stock from beans, corn, squash, peas, peppers, flowers, garlic, and herbs.

Dekśi Super is probably the one who taught me the finer principles of seed saving through lessons he shared from growing our Indian corn, *wamnaheza*, the corn we use for making *paśday-api.* For example, where I plant my corn matters. Corn can easily cross-pollinate with other corn, even a mile away. Wind carries the tiny pollen grains to the sticky silks. It is part of a two-step fertilization process and a complicated and miraculous biology lesson beyond my understanding. But the takeaway is that corn is highly susceptible to cross-pollination. Our place is situated on a bluff overlooking the vast Minnesota River valley—lands that were originally prairie. From the east edge of my garden, I can see at least three giant fields belonging to neighboring farmers who rotate crops between corn and soybeans. Yet, directly across from our garden is prairie, with portions that will soon host a solar farm. On the north side of my garden plot stands a thick row of giant pines, spruces, and brush. To the west side is our home and back yard that drops down to woods that lead to the creek below. And the south side of our garden catches just a part of our house. While occasionally I will have a random ear of Indian corn that contains a kernel or two of what looks like field corn, I feel relatively safe planting corn, especially as I move the corn farther into the garden and away from the eastern edge, where it might catch field corn pollen blowing from the south. Another way that I work to avoid cross-pollination is by observing the nearby crop rotations. Farmers who plant corn one year typically plant beans the following, which is then safe for me to plant my corn without too much concern. I also rotate growing Indian corn and Dakota popcorn every other year and have on occasion grown heirloom sweet corn. Another way one could deter cross-pollination is to know the amount of time it takes for corn to silk. If the days are different between them, there is less chance that the pollination times will coincide. Once pollen is airborne, there is a limited time that it is viable. While I do not track days to silk, I believe all these factors and the measures I do take, like rotation and changing location, decrease the possibilities of cross-pollination of field corn with my Indian corn. I know of other heirloom corn growers who take the time to hand-pollinate and cover their tassels with corn condoms. This requires some planning and labor. However, this process would be beneficial if there was a lot more exposure and potential to cross pollinate, or for those that grow more than one type of corn, or for growers that are trying to grow out seed and need to ensure purity.

I plant enough Indian corn for our family to store four to five quarts of shelled corn. This is enough to make four to five big pots of *paṡdayapi*. With a small crop as such, I am careful to pull seed from as many different cobs as possible for future planting. Yet, the quality of cobs makes a difference in seed stock. I avoid small undergrown cobs to start and pull seed from the center of cobs which tend to be larger, uniform kernels. Increasing drought conditions are revealed in the underformed and sometimes absent kernels at the top edge of the cob. One might also see evidence of insufficient water when kernels lack uniformity and show gaps or large round kernels as well. I avoid saving seed from these cobs. The other thing I do is mix seeds from previous years, again hoping to support seed diversity. Inbreeding conditions are revealed in shorter and fewer cobs—something I have seen in my biannual crops and am working to rectify. Planting at least one hundred corn stalks would help but would take up too much of my plot. Perhaps I will begin swapping corn seed with others to support diversity and reduce inbreeding.

Shelling *wamnaheza*.

One of the fun things Uncle taught me is selecting seed based on color to reveal a variety of beauty that Indian corn can generate. The kernels are shades of red, white, and blue. Some years I have planted only red and another year blue. The ears will display beautiful hues resembling beadwork. I have yet to try planting solely white one year.

Beans are another crop that I save seeds from and are relatively easy to grow. Bush beans, those under two feet tall, like kidney, Arikara Yellow, and Hopi Black Turtles, are self-pollinating. For the most part, they do not cross-pollinate unless an insect happens to pollinate across different beans at just that right moment. A miraculous self-pollinating process occurs where the plant releases pollen the night before the flowers open. The thought of this almost brings tears to my eyes. Plants being aware of day and night and self-awareness of when their own flowers will bloom! Again, science is not in my wheelhouse—I never took a biology course in my life—but the gist is that as the flower opens, the stigma brushes up against the pollen that was released, and fertilization occurs. Ta-dah!

This time of year, my table is covered with cake pans holding numerous bean varieties. I finish drying and store them for future eating. But I also save bean seeds, too, including varieties of bush, pole, and runner beans. All I do to have bean stock for future planting is to leave the pods to dry on the vine, just as I do for consumption and storage. Once the pods are dry, I shell them and dry the beans a bit more just to be sure they are fully dry. I learned the hard way when beans started molding and rotting in their storage jars. Bush beans, like Hopi Black Turtle or kidney, grow just like their name, on bushes that are about two feet high. Pole beans can grow over ten feet high and require a fence or trellis to climb. Pole beans, like Hidatsa Shield and Good Mother Stallard, tend to flower later than the bush beans and continue flowering until frost. Runner beans, like scarlet runner, also require something to climb. These beans are larger and flatter and are also referred to as butter or lima beans. Runners are considered part decorative because of their beautiful red, pink, and peach-colored flowers.

Their beauty draws in pollinators and entices me to grow them
as well. They are stunning both on the vine and in the jar. I cook
these less often, however, as they require a much longer cooking
time. Another difference between poles and runners are that pole
beans twist around fencing in a clockwise direction whereas runners climb counterclockwise. Isn't that incredible? Truly, I invariably advise new gardeners to try growing dry beans.

❖   ❖   ❖   ❖

Wild Rice, Roast, and Hominy for a Crowd

3 pounds buffalo or beef roast
1 large onion, sliced
3 cups water (and chicken broth, if desired)
2 cups wild rice
2 cups of lyed *wamnaheza*
3 tablespoons butter
salt and pepper to taste

In a roasting pan, add roast and sliced onion, and season with
salt and pepper. If roast is lean, add a bit of water to avoid
burning the meat. Bake at 350 degrees in oven for 2½ hours
or until tender. While meat is cooking, heat water. I like to
include chicken bouillon or incorporate chicken broth for half
the liquid. Rinse wild rice thoroughly. Be sure to use authentic
and Native-sourced wild rice, not black paddy rice. Add rice to
water and bring to a simmer. When rice begins to curl, cover the
pot and shut off the burner. Resist lifting the cover, leaving the
rice to finish off by steam. Wait 20–30 minutes, then drain off
any remaining liquid. In a bowl, toss rice, lyed (fully cooked)
wamnaheza. Add butter, salt, and pepper. When the roast is done
cooking, add rice and hominy. This is a delicious hearty meal.
I always sneak a small bowl of rice and hominy with the butter
and seasoning—it is so yummy!

MEDICINE

The frost advisories are upon us and so we covered our tomatoes
with old sheets. There were so many it would be a shame for them

to go to waste. Two people have claimed them and for that I am happy. I will perhaps make one more batch of bruschetta for me and my youngest son, Walker, to enjoy one last time this year.

While we managed to escape the frost, we were warned that a hard freeze is coming later this week. So, I decided I better plant the garlic cloves soon. Even though I have announced that I am not gardening next year, which is not entirely true, I still have to keep my garlic going for the following year. Besides, garlic is so easy to grow, requires little maintenance, and who can't eat forty to fifty bulbs of garlic in a year? While digging the holes and placing ends down, I thought of all the ways I use garlic. It is part of the canned spaghetti sauce, salsa, and pizza sauce recipes. It is a staple when making bruschetta, hummus, and the many hotdishes and soups I make throughout the year. But one of the most profound uses is when I was sick with Covid-19. I did what my friend Mary has done for years. I dosed myself with a clove of raw garlic per day. I chopped it up and put it in a half piece of bread and ate it. *Allium sativum*, garlic, boosts one's immune system, and studies have shown that it is stronger than leading antibiotics. That along with the elderberry syrup, cedar tea, and oregano oil might explain why I didn't end up in the hospital. In fact, I fared much better than my nineteen-year-old son at the time, whose symptoms lasted longer and were more severe. Because I love garlic, I didn't mind or really notice it seeping out of my pores and breath as Jay had mentioned.

I believe there are garlic pills one can take. But why do that when I can enjoy my home-grown garlic? The list of benefits also extends to reducing blood pressure, cholesterol, and inflammation. But one of the most interesting advantages of garlic is only gained at the immediate cutting or crushing of it, which releases sulfur compounds, including allicin. In their article "Allicin: Chemistry and Biological Properties," some smart folks (plant physiologist Jan Borlinghaus and colleagues) write, "Allicin can inhibit the proliferation of both bacteria and fungi or kill cells outright, including antibiotic-resistant strains like methicillin-resistant *Staphylococcus aureus*" (2014). That is why when my middle son came down with something, I proclaimed, "Eat raw garlic—it is good medicine!" Yes, we will eat all those garlic cloves next year.

ROLES AND RESPONSIBILITIES

Finally, the weather is starting to feel as it should. This morning is cloudy and 40 degrees. Tomorrow night, a hard freeze at 27 is predicted. I grew up in a home where waste was sinful, or I could also look at it as being resourceful; I prefer the latter. So, we have spent the past few days gathering the remaining produce from the garden. We picked at least two bushels of green tomatoes that went to friends who will watch them ripen in hopes of preserving them. One could also try those famous fried green tomatoes. I tried cooking them years ago and apparently wasn't blown away because I haven't done it since. Perhaps someone may tell me otherwise and advise me that I wasn't cooking them right or didn't season them adequately. I say, send me a recipe! We also picked a couple of gallons of remaining peppers of sorts, jalapeños, chilis from the southwest, bells, and paprikas. I was gifted these seeds from my friend Emmett, or "Shkeme" as he is more commonly known. Shkeme is a citizen of the Santa Ana Pueblo of New Mexico and is a talented artist. In addition to teaching and entertaining us through stories, he maintains the traditional songs and ceremonies of his culture. Shkem also can spit out some inspiring Native reggae music, as well as grow and feed his family and community. The chilis are just beautiful, and I am thinking of trying to make a green sauce with them.

Other than picking a few dried bean pods and a final cup of blackberries, we are now ready to put the garden to bed. We wait for the maples and oaks in our yard to drop their leaves so we can gather them up for mulch. We will spread a thick covering of leaves over the strawberry plants, newly fall-planted garlic cloves, and over a few perennial herbs. If there is enough, we will continue to cover any bare areas, first with newspaper to compost to increase organic matter in the soil. It also seems to bring more worms. Worms can improve soils on a variety of levels. Worms shred, eat, and poop decomposing organic matter, like newspaper, grass clippings, compost, thus creating casts (basically poop). Sounds gross but casts help to aerate soils, making it less compact, which helps with water and nutrient filtration. They are incredibly helpful to plants as well, because the casts are five times higher in nitrogen, seven times higher in phosphorous, and have one thousand times more bacteria than soil void of worms. Another amazing fact is that they also help clean up pollutants in soils, converting them into nontoxic particles. Yet, worms are not indigenous to our lands and originate from Europe and Asia. While I find them helpful with our clay-burdened soil, they negatively impact hardwood forests. They speed up the decomposition of fallen leaves which decreases the spongy organic layer that promotes the growth of tree seedlings, wildflowers, and ferns. We are advised by the Minnesota Department of Natural Resources to avoid introducing worms to wooded areas, especially with the invasive species of the Asian jumping worm. Yet, we are grateful for the work of the earthworms in our garden.

This year we added thicker layers of newspaper and even some cardboard to the soil. Our plan this coming growing season is to plant minimally so that we have the freedom to take a summer trip through Montana. This bucket list adventure has been delayed each year because I could not bear to part from my plant relatives. I have always shared that gardening is a way of life. For example, I need to be present for the daily picking of strawberries for the two weeks they come in. If I don't pick them daily or at least every other day, the ripening fruit draws insects, wrecking the crop. Also, picking green beans frequently signals them to produce more. And not watching the weather can lead to failing to pick dried beans before a rain that would cause them to rot. The gardening season requires I am in the garden every day and most often twice—in the morning and evening while avoiding the heat. This was why Montana has been on my bucket list for years.

✦   ✦   ✦   ✦

BBQ Beans

4 cups of prepared Good Mother Stallard beans
chopped pork hock or bacon
3 minced garlic cloves
½ cup chopped peppers (optional)
1 large onion, chopped
1 tablespoon Worcestershire sauce
1 cup BBQ sauce
1 tablespoon brown sugar
pepper
¼ cup chicken or beef broth or water

Good Mother Stallard beans work well as baked beans. Cook thoroughly but intact. You can include the bone in baking beans for added flavor. If using bacon, fry and crumble. In ceramic bean pot or Dutch oven, combine all ingredients. I add the extra bit of water/broth as these beans can start to dry up when baking. I will water down a nearly empty jar of BBQ sauce and use this for the extra moisture needed. I have also replaced a pork hock with hamburger. This dish is even tastier the second day—if it lasts that long.

UNITES RELATIVES

My southwest friend Shkeme and I have been texting and sharing photos of our respective garden bounties. Some of our crops are similar but most are different, reflective of the traditional foods we are both attempting to retain as part of our culture and diet. We also share seeds and medicines with each other, just as Indigenous peoples across Turtle Island have done for centuries.

I am full of gratitude as I admire the long green fruits that resulted from the seeds gifted by my Pueblo brother earlier in the year. I gathered the rest of the recently picked peppers and made roasted green chili sauce for the first time. I used a cornucopia of peppers but can now understand how the chilis work best for roasting. An image surfaces in my mind of the mounds of red and green chilis Shkeme and his family were roasting. The blackened, blistered skins of chilis roasted in the broiler came off much easier than the skins of bells and jalapeños. The auroras were too small and blackened to nothing, and once the skin was removed from the paprikas, only seeds and stem were left. Note to self: stick to the chilis next time when roasting and making green chili sauce. As with most of my cooking, I only loosely follow a recipe. I add garlic, chicken stock, lime juice, salt, and olive oil to the bowlful of skinned peppers. I then pour it all into a food processor and blend it into a beautiful green sauce. I had enough to fill two quart-size freezer bags. A fingertip amount revealed it was quite spicy and the tingling on my tongue reminds of the staple condiments at restaurant tables we have patronized when visiting our relatives in New Mexico. My northern tastebuds send me a reminder to dilute it when I use the green chili sauce for enchiladas.

The ability to share traditional seeds across lands and peoples is beyond gratifying. As I comb through maps of Indigenous trade routes, it is easy to see the likelihood of the long-ago exchange of foods, medicines, and knowledge between the Pueblo and Dakota peoples. My heart is full of gratitude as I think about how Shkeme and I are doing our little part to reclaim the tradition of sharing. Food does indeed unite relatives.

CALLS FOR NOURISHMENT AND FEASTING

It finally came. I woke up to the glistening frost covering the grass, deck rails, and yes, across the garden. While the coffee is brewing, I step out on the deck and into my morning ritual with a deep breath and a mini sun salutation. As I fold down to touch my toes on the frosted deck, I hear a soft sound in the still crisp air. As I gather energy from the ground and reach for the sky, I see that the sound is from one lone red leaf falling to the ground. It makes a unique crackling sound from the frost as the leaf pinballs its way down, gently hitting branches on its way down. The near semi-

Autumn Blaze maple leaves. Photograph by Tanner Peterson.

circle of autumn blaze maples in the front yard are now in their full color. And I take it all in with another breath, watching more leaves gently released from their branches.

The shift in the season puts a smile on my face. I am enjoying my breakfast looking out the big picture window. Everything is defrosting from the sunrays, and anything upright has a slight bend with the weight of residual moisture. I am full of contentment as I realize the hard labor of the season is behind us and the harvest was abundant. Just as the leaves slowly release from their mother, so, too, I begin to let go. My continual attention to plant relatives will shift to nourishment and nurturing of family, friends, and myself.

There is something about the crispness in the air that calls me to make a hearty pot of beef vegetable soup for the crew of children and grandchildren coming. We decided today is it. With the trees in full color, it is the perfect setting for family pictures amongst the blaze of autumn. I gather a few onions from our bushel basket where we store them after thoroughly drying them for weeks. I also grab a bulb of garlic from the mesh bag hanging in the laundry room. I poke my head in the "vegetable freezer" to pull out bags of green beans, carrots, and corn. I cut up a sirloin steak and use the bone to give the soup more flavor and perhaps some bone marrow. I dump in a half jar of leftover salsa, and an end-of-season tomato provides additional flavor. Other than the celery, barley, and sirloin I add, this pot of soup is a reminder of the nutritious gifts from this season's harvest. I top off this hearty meal by grabbing a loaf of frozen zucchini bread to thaw that will warm our spirits alongside the big pot of *wahaŋpi*.

It turned into the perfect autumn day we had all hoped for. Gently falling crimson leaves, sunshine, and a bit of chill in the air. We gathered pumpkins to add to the picturesque backdrop, and our middle son, serving as photographer, took the various shots between three generations of the Peterson dozen. When it became more challenging to keep the grandkids from diverting their attention from the kittens, we ended the photo shoot and headed indoors. I was grateful they came hungry, knowing Mom usually has something cooking. When I said, "Beef vegetable barley soup," I was met with mostly silence and a few comments, including, "Um, I'm probably going to just head home." Yet, I quickly prepared bowls of soup and put dabs of butter on the slices of zucchini bread and placed it all on the table. Minutes later I overheard "This is good" and "Can I have some more?" Even my "meh" son told me he liked it and shared how he just never gave soup a chance. Soon, they departed for their homes, leaving us with an empty soup pot. We were grateful because while we love soup, a big pot of soup would have left the two of us eating leftovers for a few days. We laugh together and wonder what Thanksgiving will look like and we both agreed: potluck it will be!

❖   ❖   ❖   ❖

Zucchini Bread

3 eggs
1 cup vegetable oil
2 cups sugar
2½ cups shredded zucchini
2 teaspoons vanilla
3 cups flour
1 teaspoon salt

1 teaspoon baking powder
1 teaspoon baking soda
1 tablespoon cinnamon
1 teaspoon ground cloves
1 teaspoon allspice
1 cup chopped walnuts, if desired

Beat eggs, then add oil, sugar, squash, and vanilla. Stir well. Sift dry ingredients together and add to egg mixture. Stir in nuts. Bake at 350 degrees for 1 hour or until done (insert a toothpick and when it comes out clean, it's done). This will make two large loafs. I like to make this in mini loafs and freeze them, taking out one loaf at a time.

LOSS AND HEALING

My oldest son, Hunter, and I drove northwest over to the campus of the University of Minnesota in Morris on a Friday afternoon in November. We were participating in the annual healing ceremony there. I am happy that at least one son has joined me in attending the ceremonial gatherings the past few years. The administration, with guidance from the American Indian Advisory Committee, has made a commitment to support healing in acknowledgment of its past boarding school history and the residual impacts of that era on Native students and communities. It is part of a broader vision to support Native American student education equity and postsecondary attainment. Earlier, I had helped with the campus-wide strategic planning. Acknowledgment and healing were identified as important steps in the work. One of my roles was to provide "cultural translations" for the administration. I can share that it is not easy to bring ceremony into an institutional setting. The institution's formalities, including bureaucratic policies and procedures, and explicit and hierarchical communications, collide with the sacredness of ceremony. I appreciate the extra work others had to do to set up the ceremonial fire on campus. Preparations *are* a part of ceremony and never require drawing on paperwork or policy workarounds. The commitments of the campus community have provided an opportunity for healing people and the lands that once held the Indian boarding school.

From 1887 until 1909, the Indian boarding school was operated by the Roman Catholic Sisters of Mercy and later by the U.S. government. The current Multi-Ethnic Resource Center was the former boys' dormitory and the place I spent much of my time over my five years as a student in the 1980s. Part of the annual sacred event includes thoroughly smudging down the only building remaining from that horrific era. As we walk through it, I think of the children who were likely forced to be there and the moms and dads, the grandparents, and all the families that longed for their return. This includes my grandpa's siblings, a story I only recently uncovered.

The lands where the University of Minnesota, Morris sits are original Dakota lands. The waters of the Pomme de Terre River flow nearby. I have no understanding of the French language, beyond *oui* and some of the French surnames that made their way into our Dakota family, like LaBatte and LaFromboise. I learned that *pomme de terre* translates as "potato" and literally as "apples of the earth." And we know that *Mni Sota Makoce,* the land that our state is named for, is blanketed with Dakota names, further providing evidence that these are Dakota homelands. Pomme de Terre River was originally called Owobopte Wakpa. Many Dakota place-names describe the relationship we have had with Mother Earth and all her creation. Owobopte Wakpa is the river where the wild turnips are dug. *Tipsiŋna* (wild turnips), or prairie potato, were abundant in this area and were dug up as a staple food. The Anishinaabe, too, had a similar naming in their language for this place, Opinikani Zibi, the wild potatoes river. I am told *tipsiŋna* is found in open prairies on south-facing hillsides in gravelly or sandy dry soils.

The scientific name for *tipsiŋna* is *Pediomelum esculentum.* I learn that the fuzzy blue and purple flowers that bloom during the early summer months help in locating the plant. The hairy stems, approximately twelve inches high, have multiple branches with five erect oval leaves. The fiber, vitamins C and B6, potassium, magnesium, iron, and calcium it provides indeed made it a diet staple. The tuberous root is used as a vegetable and a flavoring for soup, and it also can be pounded into a powder to be used as flour or to thicken soups.

I have cooked with *tipsiŋna* from a braid gifted to me, but I most often use store-bought turnips in lieu of the wild turnips. Searching for and digging wild turnips remains on my exploration list. But after some quick research, I am quite sure I have seen the plant on my hikes and will search for it in the coming summer. I have also tried growing turnips in my garden, and the results were pitiful. I suspect I started them too late. Turnips, along with ruta-bagas, meat, and our beautiful Indian corn, make our traditional soup, *paṡdayapi*. The word *paṡdayapi* translates as "they make it bald." It refers to the process of turning the hard, flint-like corn into hominy. This method requires lye, derived by adding hard wood ash to water. I have heard a scientist describe the natural chemical process, nixtamalization, but it is alchemy to me. What I do know is this.

I make *paṡdayapi* only on special occasions. I start by taking a quart of the Dakota corn I grew out of my freezer. I only store my corn in the freezer because I once had a moth infestation. It was likely from the bean pods I bring into my house each year. Note to self: another reason I ought to take up Buffalo Bird Woman's method of threshing beans. The moths got into my corn, flour, and boxes of baking items. The sight of little baby off-white squirmy worms got the better of me, and I threw away a garbage bag of infested goods. The experience brought back a memory of my grandma. She was known for baking bread. On occasion, my *Ice-paŋṡi* (female cousins) and I would help her in the kitchen. We would hunt for her big bread-making bowls in the unheated porch off the kitchen. Then we would help make the dough by measuring out weevil-filled flour. Us girls looked sideways at each other after pointing out the little bugs, which she dismissed as something inconsequential. Perhaps my grandma could not afford to throw out her flour every time a little moth ventured into her kitchen. There were, after all, eight children, numerous grandchildren, and the friends and relatives that she fed and nurtured with her delicious bread loaves, buns, and fry bread. She would likely have scolded me for throwing out my things. The corn I had tenderly nurtured for six months, from planting the kernels to shelling the dried corn from their cobs was wasted. And so today, I bag the corn into quart bags and freeze it—the perfect amount for a sixteen-quart soup pot.

One of the first steps is to, in fact, make the corn kernels bald. That is, the corn must soften, and the outer hull gets sloughed off in the process. I start with taking out my old white enamel pot I keep stored in the garage. I picked it up at a secondhand shop, wanting a pot just for this next step. From a reused coffee can, I measure out about 1½ cups of the hard wood ash I obtained from Dekśi. He still burns wood to heat his house. True, so do my parents, and I could easily get this from my dad's stove as well. But I prefer to ask Dekśi so that he knows I am still making the treasured soup he taught me to make, along with growing the Dakota corn, a gift he gave from his own seed stock. He has shared that when he reincarnates, he wants to smell the familiar aroma and eat bowlfuls of *paśdayapi.* He has shared this corn with many people, as have I, so it will likely continue. Rest assured, Dekśi, at least the next generation is making this traditional soup—I have at least one son who knows how to make it.

After about two to three hours, I can smell the familiar aroma. The corn has started to shed the outer hull and is starting to puff up. This process allows the absorption of niacin or B3 when consumed, an important vitamin for brain functioning and more. While the corn is cooking, I bring out my big soup pot. This is the pot I use when I want to feed a large gathering of people or make *paśdayapi* for friends and family. This, too, I gather from the garage and wipe off the summer dust that has settled in from the prairie winds. I add a beef soup bone to water. To me it doesn't matter which bone, but I know that Dekśi prefers beef ribs. Of course, this soup was originally made with buffalo and if one has the opportunity, this would be a more authentic version. The bones provide flavor and nutrition. Wisdom like this eventually circulates throughout the generations. Today, I see that one can purchase bone broth in half-quart plastic containers, marketed as a superfood to support hair, skin, nail, and gut health. While that starts cooking, I cube up about three pounds of beef or venison roast. After adding the meat to the pot, I then peel and chop two turnips and a large rutabaga. Turnips and rutabaga require some patience. The peeling takes time and then a heavy-duty knife is required to chop up the firm rutabaga. Here, too, Uncle and I each have our preferences: he cuts chunks; I prefer to dice mine into relatively smaller pieces. Keep it all cooking on medium heat, at a nice simmer like I would any other soup.

When I think the corn might be done, I pick a kernel or two out, rinse thoroughly and taste, checking that the corn is soft but not mushy. Then the rinsing begins. This process requires diligence. According to my research, lye or sodium hydroxide can cause severe damage to our insides and even cause death. Mom apparently didn't know this when my brother and I got soap in our mouths for swearing or sassing. The alkali solution's caustic properties are used in making soaps and cleaners. I continue to scan literature and find out that food-grade lye is actually used to cure olives. Who would have known? I love olives! It is also used in making lutefisk from whitefish and for giving pretzels the accustomed dark and shiny shell. Okay, maybe lye isn't that dangerous after all. While there are many uses for lye, I remain cautious since I read that lye and aluminum can cause things to explode. Additionally, I remember my grandma advising me to rinse my ashes outside with the garden hose as they can wreck drainpipes. I followed her directions for years until Jay assured me that it is safe to wash ashes down today's plastic pipes. Even with all this information, I still rinse my lyed corn several times until the water runs clear.

I continue to grow *wamnaheza*, originally from the corn seed that Uncle gave me, and have gifted corn seed from my stock to many people. The list of folks includes the students in the Native American garden program at the University of Minnesota, Morris, my alma mater. The students were delighted and curious about the corn, as well as the numerous bean varieties I provided while sharing my gardening practices and secrets with them. I am always excited to talk beans, heirloom tomatoes, and more with the students whether it is on campus or when they have visited my plot, or more recently via Zoom—thanks, pandemic. One such engagement stands out for me. Mary Jo, the campus healthy eating coordinator at the time, who helped coordinate the campus Native gardens, invited me out to her farm kitchen to demonstrate how to make *paśdayapi* and seed save. Students and faculty advisers from the Native Garden club, the Circle of Indigenous Nations Association (CINA), and the campus chapter of the American Indian Science and Engineering Society (AISES) were all invited. The event was even recorded and shared as an AISES activity. Thinking about the teaching and coordination of the preparations involved, I was able to solicit Jay and *miciŋksipi* (my sons) to help.

After introductions and some brief storytelling, we set out to give the students directions. We attempted to spread out bodies at the various stations. I put Jay and the boys on the meat-cutting station to navigate all the knives required and avoid any devastating issues at a university-sponsored event. One of the students secured buffalo for the soup. What a rare treat for us as we typically have access only to beef or venison. I had students shell some of the corn that had been braided and hung to dry and quickly got the corn cooking in ash as this takes the most time. Other students began preparing the vegetables. Mary Jo asked me to give some direction to the students on the practices of seed saving. A bit too late, I joined the students who were laughing and already had shelled most of the corn. Still, I gave a quick lesson with the remaining unshucked cobs on seed selection to ensure quality and diversity of seed. The day went by quickly. Soon we were feasting on *paśdayapi*, black bean hummus, fresh tomatoes, and more. I think back on this day and wonder if the students grasped the profundity of the event—a university whose history as an Indian boarding school had worked to eradicate the Nativeness out of the Native students of that time was coming full circle by restoring

Native foods and gardening, language, and traditions with Native students today. It is an incredible contribution to working to make things right.

I am pleased with the continued healing and efforts to restore made by the university. When I attended Morris back in the late 1980s, there was significant support to help me succeed in graduating. Mike Miller was the Native adviser then—an Anishinaabe from the White Earth Reservation whose office was a daily drop-in for me. Sheri, my first campus friend, was from there too. She and I, along with other minority students, attended their bridge program. It was a summer program that acclimated students of color to campus by enabling us to establish relationships and gain a few credits before our freshman year. NASA—the Native American Student Association—was our own version of CINA. It provided activities and promoted camaraderie among the sixty or so Natives back then. Today, there are more than three hundred Native students attending Morris! Leadership from the American Indian Advisory Committee to the chancellor has guided the administration as it provides support services and improves the campus environment for students. The late Mike Miller, a one-person show back in my day, has been replaced by at least eight staff members through the Native American Student Success Program.

For the past several years, the campus has held an annual ceremony. Acknowledging the harm the Indian Boarding School inflicted, remembering the children who died there, and naming the trauma that era brought to Native families and communities are all significant aspects of the sacred event. The university has provided space for the campus community to recognize how this history impacts our communities and work to reconcile—to make things right so that students today and tomorrow have a positive educational experience. Beyond the yearly event, the school provides numerous activities and initiatives, including language revitalization, student support services, and integrating history and truth telling across curricula and the campus environment. We have a long way to go toward healing and reconciliation across our region, *Mni Sota*, and country. Yet I am encouraged by the pathway the university and others have begun to walk, recognizing the loss and harm, and centering healing.

✦   ✦   ✦   ✦

Paṡdayapi

2–3 quarts water to start
1 quart *wamnheza*
1½ cup hard wood ash
beef bones
3 pounds roast
2 small–medium rutabagas
2 turnips
4 tablespoons salt
1 tablespoon pepper
1 tablespoon chili powder
1/8 teaspoon cayenne pepper

Fill pot with water, *wamnaheza,* and ash. Bring to a simmer and cook for approximately three hours or until outer hull is sloughed off and corn is puffed up. Rinse a kernel and taste to ensure softness. Rinse lyed corn repeatedly until completely free of ash. In large soup pot, add bones, cubed beef roast (or venison or buffalo). Peel and cube or dice rutabagas and turnips and add to pot. Add seasonings. Bring to a boil and turn heat down to a simmer and cook for two to three hours or until vegetables are soft. Of course, my grandma would have added only salt and pepper, but I like the additional seasonings that Dekṡi suggested.

SUSTAINS

I was visiting with a group of university students enrolled in a Sustainability Leadership course. It is always fun to engage with young minds—it causes me to be hopeful about our future, despite all the environmental calamities under way. Their sharing about how they see the world and their curiosity about what it means to be mindful and to live in sustainable and regenerative ways gives me optimism about these future decision makers. After reading a few passages with them, I asked, "What are some of the ways you are

Prairie buttercup along the trail.

reclaiming your relationship with land and what is a tradition you are maintaining and honoring?" Their answers were profoundly simple: "lying in the grass," "appreciating all the land provides me," and "taking mindful walks along the prairie grasses." The conversation is reflective, drawing on childhood memories of making treasured family dishes and their desire to carry on those traditions and recipes. The students share stories of family members coming together to cook and celebrate holidays. They talk about recipes and foods and how they knit together relationships and sustain family. Our group discussion affirmed for me that gardening and ceremony support sustaining us collectively—*oyate owasiŋ*. Gardening practices support sustaining body, mind, and spirit, a factor I personally have noticed. Yet, their impact extends beyond people and the next generations. Mindful gardening practices also sustain land and water, which is the basis and connection to our existence. Our collective body of understanding how we live, how we grow food, how we come together, how we carry out rituals, traditions, and ceremonies sustains the rich cultural fibers of each of us. Our families—just like the diversity of place shapes the taste of our plant relatives—save us from homogeneity and nurture the organic fiber of our humanity.

SUSTENANCE

We all have heard about how the pandemic revealed longstanding disparities, including a failed foodway system and many other broken systems. On the news I observe long lines of cars snaking across our cities as people struggle to find food for their families. Food pantries are overwhelmed, seeing triple the number of usual patrons. Many, we hear, are making use of this assistance for the first time. The food shortages and empty shelves in our supermarkets, the supply chain bogged down out at sea, the unemployment, stay-at-home orders, and schooling in homes all contributing to the increasing demand for food. Food, what many of us take for granted, was now insecure. People were and are hungry.

There were also those who took an opportunity to take up growing their own food. They began to purchase seeds, equipment, and gardening supplies until there was a shortage of those too. Our family couldn't find canning lids to purchase except for those priced exorbitantly online from those taking advantage of the skewed supply and demand. Food sovereignty is the ability of the people to control the systems and mechanisms to produce, distribute, and consume food. It is having the ability to feed oneself, instead of relying upon the corporate food system. Food sovereignty gained traction across households, communities, and tribes.

Guiltily, I shared with Jay that I had never experienced hunger in my life. Sure, I've been hungry momentarily, knowing I would be eating soon. Or by choice I have gone to bed a bit hungry during the early stages of a diet when my body is getting used to reduced calories. Even during my childhood, I don't recall ever being hungry. While I may have been deprived of trendy and designer clothes and shoes, I grew up on a farm where food was never an issue. We raised hogs, chickens, cattle, and had a garden that pro-

The barn at the farm from my childhood.

vided plenty of food. The basement stored my mother's canned goods in our one-hundred-year-old house. Several shelves held peaches, stewed tomatoes, corn, and even boiled chickens. Dad was and remains an avid hunter, so our diet also included venison and waterfowl. I hold images and memories of butchering chickens and defeathering geese, ducks, and pheasants. I can still recall the process, including the tree stump that held the chopped heads of chickens, the hot water that helped to remove feathers, the job of cleaning gizzards, and the handheld blowtorch to singe remaining pinfeathers. I also hold harvest memories of digging potatoes out of the garden, including a time spent in the rain to save the potatoes before the weather turned to snow. I have canning memories of my hands placing peach pits in the bottom of wide-mouth quart jars before filling them with peeled and halved peaches. When I started my own canning, I asked Mom why we had to include the pit since we would never eat it. She simply replied, "Because that's what my mom did."

Butchering chickens at the farm: Mom, brother Rob, Dad, and extended family.

Today my own basement shelves are stocked with salsa, tomato soup, spaghetti sauce, jellies, and pie filling. Our freezers are full of green beans, kale, carrots, and berries. And our kitchen counter is full of jars of several varieties of heirloom beans, Dakota popcorn, and dehydrated pears and apples. Nourishing foods are abundant in our home.

We are a country of wealth and poverty, people who are overweight and hungry, abundance and scarcity. The continuum between food insecurity and food sovereignty stretches across people and place. I am encouraged by the tribal communities and families who are embracing food sovereignty, by raising buffalo, harvesting wild rice, and building greenhouses. Yet, I wonder who will continue to grow their own food after the pandemic is no longer the center of the news. Will we have changed society's food systems? Will we continue to provide opportunities for families to adopt sustainable approaches that support local and family food sovereignty?

Wild Rice Bowl for One

1 cup cooked wild rice
⅓ cup cooked tepary beans
¼ cup chopped red pepper
12 cherry tomatoes, halved
2 tablespoons chopped red onion
½ cup arugula
1 tablespoon feta cheese

Simple Lemon Dressing
1 lemon, juiced
2–3 tablespoons extra virgin olive oil
1 tablespoon balsamic vinegar
1 tablespoon honey
pepper

There are times that I cannot entice Jay to join me in one of my meals. He'll say, "Looks too funky for me." This is one of those dishes, but I have to say . . . it is delicious! Vigorously shake dressing ingredients together. Taste and adjust as needed (remember, measurements listed are approximate—I'm one of those cooks who eyeballs amount). Toss all the ingredients together and enjoy!

Wild rice bowl for one.

SHARING DELIGHT

The other day, I motored to Ma and Dad's place, a few acres off a gravel road, just seven miles from us. To get there, I travel across the Wakpamnisota, then back up out of the valley. When I was younger, Mom tended the garden, but today my dad is the gardener. He grows cucumbers, dill, cabbage, carrots, onions, and a few tomato plants that I seed each year. I am especially grateful that he grows the cucumbers so that we can make pickles each year. I make four big commercial size jars of baby dills and sliced pickles that I store in our second refrigerator. Mom taught me how to make pickles without canning them. They are made with a hot brine poured over the cucumbers, dill, and garlic; the jar sits on the countertop for a couple of days and then is stored in a refrigerator for the year. I have found that using jars instead of the plastic ice-cream pails Ma uses holds the crispness of the pickles longer. Each year, Dad has more cucumbers than we can collectively eat, fresh or pickled. So, in addition to inviting people to my garden for extra produce, I take people to my dad's patch of cukes. Recently, one of my former high school students from back in the day was invited to pick cukes. Joe, his wife, Brittany, and their brood of children followed me up to Ma and Dad's. At least four or five children, ranging from three years old to twelve, leaped from their van once we arrived. Together we picked enough cucumbers for them to make three gallons of pickles and as I understand, they ate them up in a matter of days.

✦   ✦   ✦   ✦

Two-Day Dill Pickles
cucumbers
6 cups water
3 cups white vinegar
3 tablespoons sugar
3 tablespoons canning salt
8 heads of dill
4 garlic cloves

Source some big glass jars: the one-gallon size is perfect. Sometimes I find these in secondhand or antique shops. Ma and Dad use ice-cream pails, but I believe glass jars help hold the crunchiness of pickles longer. Start your brine in a pot on the stove by combining the water, white vinegar, canning salt, and sugar. Bring it to a simmer while preparing cukes. Clean the cucumbers, removing dirt and pricklies. Place 4 heads of dill and 4 cloves of garlic on the bottom of the jar. Pack the jar with the cukes. I use different-size cucumbers but slice large ones for making a jar of slicers. Leave just enough room for 4 more heads of dill. Make sure you have a towel or potholder under jar. When brine has come to a simmer, remove from heat, and pour over dill and cukes to the top of the jar. Secure and tighten cover. Leave on the counter for two full days. Then refrigerate for up to a year. We have a second refrigerator for adding three-to-four gallon jars of pickles to enjoy throughout the year.

Wakpamnisota.

PROVIDES COMFORT

Yesterday my son Hepaŋna and I attended the funeral of a young person. It was a traditional ceremony attended by a large crowd, including many people beyond the small community. It was quite sad and emotional for me, thinking of the impact on the parents of losing a child the same age as one of my own. The ceremony was quite different from the mainstream funerals where mourners primarily sit and passively listen. The traditional Dakota ceremony required engagement from those gathered, listening intently to the words and instructions from the spiritual leaders. As the four directions song was sung by the drum group, we collectively moved our bodies in near unison west, north, east, south, looking to the skies above, and to Mother Earth below our feet. After additional songs and guiding words, each of us gathered a handful of soil to sprinkle over the family's child, sibling, grandchild, fellow community member, lost future leader, and

Fallen Autumn Blaze maple leaves. Photograph by Tanner Peterson.

collective relative. One of the spiritual helpers smudged each of us with one of our medicines—*pejiȟota.* Then we attempted to bring comfort to those closest to the loved one lost. Yet it was clear the exchange was reciprocal. We were being medicine for each other.

I elected not to attend the community meal as the crowd and time was and would be significant but had made something for my own family to gather around. Hepaŋ and I rejoined his brother and dad at home for a meal. After hours of discussion, supporting each other, and hugs the boys left. With the house now quiet, I joined Jay, our beloved *šuŋka* (dog), and our two unnamed kittens in the garden. I looked out at the trees that were now nearly bare and shifted my gaze in front of me, to the huge piles of red, orange, and burgundy leaves, their blaze now muted. With Jay's diligent work over the past days, half the garden was covered with fallen leaves gathered from the maple trees. The soils, spent plants, perennials, and recently planted garlic cloves were preparing for the cold days ahead. It was time to rest in the cradle of our mother. I gathered a tub of the leaves, patting them down, with my thoughts. I thought about the young person who collectively the community had joined together in preparing for the next season—the next leg of their journey. *Mitakuye owasiŋ.*

SHARING GRIEF

The swapping of meals and produce is common between my parents and us. Whether veggies, pumpkin bars, or hotdishes, we like to share because we are both two-people households, which is more challenging to cook and bake for. During one of these sharing days, I brought them the remaining cabbage heads Jay had retrieved from the garden while preparing beds for the winter. They were small outgrowths of the original plant but still edible and later Dad shared his gratitude as his cabbages did not make it. He will clean and freeze them for his famous winter bushwhacker's stew. It is a hearty venison vegetable stew made from his annual deer hunt and our collective homegrown vegetables.

I timed my visit to meet tribal historic preservation officers at my parents' house. The officers were invited to make plans for a collection of stone artifacts my stepgrandpa had acquired during his career in a gravel company. As I understand the story, he would grab rocks that looked like they told a story off the conveyer belt before they went to the crusher. The collection is in a five-gallon pail that Dad inherited upon my stepgrandpa's passing. Dad had asked me to help him find an appropriate home for them. Cheyanne was the first to arrive. I have known Cheyanne for many years and immediately recognized her tall slender form, her dark hair, and lightly freckled face emerging from an SUV. She is a relative, perhaps a fourth cousin on my maternal grandfather's side. In her typical deliberate and thoughtful manner, she shares a brief story. She tells of her search for Mom's house and how she initially drove past the grove that hides my parents' home. She continues to share how she had turned around after recognizing she had driven past the desired location. She headed east again on the gravel road, traveling slowly when she spotted something in the field. She describes how she rolled her window down to see if she could determine if it was a deer when she heard a cat crying. She then shows us a picture of the crying gray cat on her cell phone.

Miss Kitty! We are sure it is Mom and Dad's reliable mouse catcher who had been missing for two days. She explains that she is at the edge of the road. I threw my coat and gloves on and trot down the driveway and find her in the same spot Cheyanne described. "Oh my God, Kitty!" I tenderly picked her up and ran back to the house. Assessing her now, I see the gruesome level of damage to her. One bloody empty eye socket and the other side, a dangling eyeball covered in black dried blood, and a garbled mouth that seemed to be missing pieces. I can hardly look at her. I close my eyes and cry out, "Mom, she needs to go to a vet." Mom is crying and trying to call my dad, who is deer hunting up at my brother's place. I ask Cheyanne to call a local vet's office and her voice fades out because all I can hear is the cat's loud meow cry. Sitting on the deck steps, I rock her and talk to her soothingly as best I can between my and Mom's sobbing. The cat's instinctive motor begins purring, despite her gurgling breathing sound and the meow cry she lets out every five seconds. I understand now that Miss Kitty will not make it.

"Mom, call Jay, she isn't going to make it. She's in a lot of pain." I can hear her leaving him a message and remember Jay is like me, he rarely has his ringer on. I asked Cheyanne to grab my phone in the house and call Jay. Miraculously he answers and I cry out the bare story. As we wait for relief to come, I ask Mom if she wants to hold Kitty. She declines and I understand as the cat's face looks nothing like Miss Kitty. The fifteen minutes trying to bring a tiny bit of comfort to a beloved cat feels like an eternity. I look around at her little shingled cat house on the deck Dad had made for her, along with a little breezeway to cut down on the howling winter winds.

Mom returned from inside the house; she was able to reach Dad and share the devastating news. Still crying, she begins to tell stories of Miss Kitty. Dad, a dog man, never liked cats until they moved here. Soon, he was cutting up meat for her and setting out nightly leftovers. She continues, "Miss Kitty followed Bob around, out to his garage to work on cars, and walked with him down to the mailbox, and over to the wood pile to cut and gather wood for the stove." Miss Kitty was like Dad's former dog companions, faithful and loving. Having a good cat or two around is important to those that live in the country, since they keep mice out of the house, the surrounding buildings, and the gardens. Miss Kitty filled that role of a reliable mouser and more. Jay took care of Miss Kitty, assuming the task of ending her pain. Then he tenderly wrapped her in one of her blankets and buried her next to one of the pine trees on the edge of the yard that overlooks a field sure to be filled with mice. Mother Earth, too, holds and comforts one of God's creations that I accept is part of life's journey. I am grateful for the kindness and mercy Cheyanne and Jay shared that heartbreaking day.

Upon Dad's return, I explained how she came to her demise. "I believe it was a hawk, or perhaps an eagle." But Dad doesn't accept this idea. "No, I'm sure someone ran her over," he countered. It was perhaps months later that Dad's explanation for her early death sinks in. She was found on the edge of the road. Her grue-some facial distortion was likely caused by an oncoming vehicle. A raptor wouldn't have left her at the edge of the road to die. All of these clues now make sense. Having learned of the food cycle during my school days, it was easier for me to accept that Miss Kitty's misfortune was due to an attempt for a good meal by a big bird, rather than a thoughtless or intentionally cruel act by a person. Rest in peace, Miss Kitty.

MESSY

I recently passed by a farm on a road to town. It is a place I never could get a feel for as I drove by because enormous trees blocked it from view. However, on this day I did a double take. A big white house stood bold against the brown tilled land. The area sur-rounding the home was now void of trees and grasses. Of course, I do not know the reasons for denuding this plot, but a sadness came over me as I began recounting the number of newly bull-dozed groves or small patches of trees cut down in the area over the past couple of years. No evidence of trees remained, only neatly expanded, plowed fields.

As I continued my drive, I began counting the number of fields that were already plowed up for next year's planting season. Harvest season is now mostly complete, yet some farmers start plowing up their fields in advance, exposing the rich dark soil. Perhaps half of the fields on the drive to town were unplowed with remnants of corn stalks or bean plants left behind after the combines had done their job of harvesting. My dad, a farmer for much of his life, shared that leaving a little "trash" on the field aids in preventing soil erosion. Trash is what I remember him call-ing it, and the word fits when spent plants like corn, beans, and residue are left in the fields after harvest. The roots of the plant remain in the ground, which holds in the soil. This is especially important when the prairie winds begin howling in the coming winter. Whiteout conditions—fine snow blowing so hard that a person cannot see to drive—are common here in our area. The loss of groves and trees here and there also impacts winter visibility. It's like driving through one giant flat field for miles with nothing to slow down the blowing snow. Snow fences are now being put up to aid in preventing huge drifts from building up on roads and I keep thinking, Why didn't we have the foresight to just keep some trees and vegetation here and there? Yet there is something worse than snow drifts because of cleared vegetation.

Snirt. Snirt is a mix of snow and dirt that ends up in road ditches. What makes snirt so damaging is that it is made up of topsoil that has blown off the plowed fields. Topsoil is full of nutrients and organic matter, including phosphorous. When spring returns and snow begins to melt, what remains ends up in our waterways through runoff. What happens when phosphorous is added to creeks, rivers, and lakes? According to the Environmental Protection Agency, increased phosphorous feeds algae, creating algae blooms, which in turn decreases dissolved oxygen. This harmful process is called eutrophication. Again, I am no scientist, but I do remember that living things require oxygen.

I am curious to know why a simple method to prevent soil erosion is not a more common practice. Is it our desire to tidy things up and make everything look neat? Perhaps our impatience and future orientation cause us to prime the fields and gardens for next spring. After all, our society has deemed that *time is money*, and if we can just start planting earlier, we can have a longer growing season and perhaps increase our chance for bumper crops. I think about the potential consequences of our collective shortsightedness—when we evaluate and make decisions solely through an economic lens. Sure, economics may need to be factored in, but we can and should include environmental factors.

Several sustainability practices are gaining momentum as we continue to learn about the effects of soil erosion. No-till gardening and planting, cover crops, creating wind breaks (like trees), mulching, and leaving residue ("trash") all help to prevent soil erosion. Let's embrace patience, and the messy and untidy—and stop the snirt.

FAMILY

Every other year, the branches of the apple trees hang heavy with fruit. And every year, the apples have been loaded with apple maggot and codling moth infestation. It is beyond disappointing. Jay has tried different approaches, including the eco-friendly applications of neem oil. This year, after the blossoms fell and little fruits emerged—allowing the pollinators to do their work—he regularly applied an organic insecticide to the apple trees and still hung coffee cans of apple cider vinegar from each tree to serve as insect trap. He also picked up all the apples from the June drop and the many apples that fell because of extremely dry weather. This, we understand, also decreases the infestation of damaging insects. We still had some buggy apples, but the infestation was minimal. We could finally enjoy the Honeycrisp, Golden Delicious, and an unknown early apple. I'll just say, despite the significant apple drop from dry conditions, we had more apples than we knew what to do with from our four apples trees. Ma and Dad made applesauce, and I dehydrated apple slices because jars of applesauce from a few years ago remain in the basement. We saved the best apples to eat, carefully selecting, cleaning, and bagging them to store in the second refrigerator. Still, we had apples, and I asked Jay what else we could do with them. He then shared fond childhood memories of eating apple butter on toast. So, I set out to make apple butter for the first time. It took me two days to finish but was well worth it, since Jay exclaimed after that first spoonful that it was better than his memories. Apple butter will be added to our special value-added apple activities, including making apple cider and pies.

Jay and I worked together, cleaning apples for days ahead of the designated cider day. It takes a lot of apples to make cider and fortunately we had them. I couldn't ask my parents to help this year, so I attempted to lure our boys over to help with a promise to order pizza from the local winery. Two of our sons agreed to help with chopping numerous bushels of apples. Jay ran the cider press while the boys and I worked diligently to fill buckets of chopped apples, never keeping up. I kept smiles to myself as I witnessed Hepaŋna eating slices when his chopping slowed. Caske would disappear from the table set up outside, fascinated by how the contraption pressed the juice out of the apples. We visited some but it was mainly a quiet, mindful affair so we wouldn't chop our fingers off. Eager bees would be found floating in the pitcher of freshly pressed cider. Jay would use a strainer to pour the cider into empty plastic juice containers my dad saved for the affair. Finally, we each took a swig from the jug to taste the freshest, most magnificent flavor. The boys were certainly impressed and thought that maybe the work was indeed worth it. After two hours of chopping, we took a break away from the buzzing insects that were drunk on apples and headed indoors to enjoy the pizza break. The second leg of the work required a bit more motivation. After four hours of chopping, I could sense the boys were getting restless. Hepaŋ was the first to throw in the towel. I handed him a jug of the amber-colored cider, hugged him, and thanked him for helping. Then, Jay started in with comments of giving up. "We took the time to clean all these apples. That was a lot of work," I declared in response. While I finished solo chopping the last half bushel of apples, Caske helped by hauling in chairs and taking empty bushel baskets to the garage. *Kitaŋȟ!* Finally, the last apple was in sight. Altogether, we made twelve gallons of cider. We could have bought the apple cider at Walmart for about seven dollars per gallon. I don't need to do the math to know that we could never sell cider. After distributing cider to our helpers, my parents, and gifting a few, we froze six jugs of cider for ourselves that will surely not make it through the year.

❖   ❖   ❖   ❖

Apple Butter

a lot of apples
1 cup brown sugar
1 cup maple syrup
1 tablespoon cinnamon
1 teaspoon nutmeg

recipe continued ▶

1 teaspoon ground cloves
vanilla or maple extract

Heat oven to 350 degrees. Fill one of those white-speckled black
enamel roasters with chopped unpeeled apples. It is the kind
I cook a turkey in. Bake until the apples are soft and can be easily
mashed. It will take approximately an hour. After mashing the
apples, add to a big slow cooker and turn on low with the cover
off for about 10–12 hours. I did this step the next day to start in
the early in the morning. After perhaps five hours, begin adding
flavorings and stir. Continue to stir throughout the day. I started
test tasting during the last few hours and added more sugar and
seasoning as desired. It is ready to process into jars once it has
reduced to a thick spreadable consistency. Meanwhile, sterilize
small jelly jars and gather canning supplies. Fill jars, leaving an
inch of space on top. Top with 2–3 drops of lemon juice if desired
to ensure adequate acidity. Be sure to wipe the jar lips before
topping with heated lids and rings. Process for 5–10 minutes.
For jars that do not seal, place in the refrigerator. This is so delicious on toast!

Apple Pie Filling

6 quarts apples
lemon juice
2–3 cups sugar
½ cup flour
4 tablespoons cinnamon
2 teaspoons nutmeg

I make this pie filling for about three pies at a time. I am not a
rule follower, so the amounts are approximate. As Dad used the
apple peeler, which peeled, cored, and spiral sliced the apples at
once, I would move them into a big bowl, sprinkle them with
some lemon juice, and stir. When there were about 6 quarts of
sliced apples, I would prepare the other ingredients in a small
bowl, stir, and add to the apples. I would taste test and add more
sugar and seasonings if needed. Then, I would baste the bottom
of a pie crust with whisked egg wash. This helps prevent soggy-
bottom crusts. Add the pie filling. I like to top with a few pats of

Jay rolls out pie crusts and Mom puts apple pies together.

butter before adding the top crust. Pinch the edges together and, with a knife, add a cute design to create ventilation for when the pie will be in the oven. You can also baste with egg wash and sprinkle cinnamon and sugar on top if desired. We wrapped our pies in layers of plastic wrap and tinfoil before adding them to freezer bags. Be sure to freeze pies in one layer so as not to crush the crusts. Bake the pies at 350 degrees for about an hour. The crust should be golden. I typically place a cookie sheet under the pie to avoid bubbling pie filling spilling in the oven. There is nothing like pulling a hot apple pie out of the oven for your guests. But be assured: a slice of warm apple pie can be eaten for your breakfast as well.

I recently pulled the last apple pie filling from the basement. The two jars had dates written in marker on the lid. Good grief—they were from four years ago! I made apple bars with them, and it was nearly as delicious as a fresh jar of pie filling. It was definitely time to restock. Some years we can pie filling with my parents, and other years we freeze whole pies. The great thing about pie filling is you can make a lot, and it can last for years. Making pies to freeze is a lot more work, yet it is easy to pull one out for baking. But you eat the few of them up in a year and then it starts all over again. This year, we went for pies and as is our tradition, we set up the makeshift factory with Ma and Dad.

When we preserve foods together, we each take an assigned task that is aligned with our skills. My mom makes beautiful pie crusts and so she would make the dough. Unfortunately, she was still recovering from her chest being cut open for open-heart surgery. The muscles needed to roll dough out into thin circles were assigned to Jay. I was surprised he agreed. It was endearing to watch my mom give him instructions and encouragement. She is a patient teacher. Dad was assigned to the apple peeler. He likes working with equipment; perhaps it is reminiscent of his farming days. I made the filling and once Mom put the bottom crusts into the collection of pie plates, I filled them with scoops of sweetened and spiced filling. She would follow with the top crust and delicately carve a little tree on top for design. Together, we made a dozen apple pies. After dividing them between the two households, we carefully placed them into the already full freezers. Now, we are ready for winter. Our family and friends will enjoy the abundant harvest of fruits and vegetables that will nourish our family through the cold and dark months ahead.

Waniyetu

Seeding Another Generation

Warmth and coolness entangle.
She emanates, children birth, reaching heavenward.

Another mother's hand nudges
stirs and wakens.
Hand from hand they come,
Spanning across time,
delivered to this very moment.
Sown and cradled
nurtured in faith, they emerge
from cherished tears suckled
and solar rays transformed.

Stretching to reach the heavens
to nourish and sustain
families of past,
protected by a grandmother's embrace
yields a future promise discovered.

Winter
The Time When the Snow Lives

RECALLS SACRED MOMENTS

We have entered the tree popping moon—*Caŋkapopa Wi*. It is December and there is no snow on the ground—in fact, it rained yesterday. I am grateful for the rain as it had been a long stretch without any moisture. My body sends signals when a lack of moisture has moved to a whole new level. My hair begins to straighten and loses all texture, I start getting nosebleeds, and my skin resembles a parched desert landscape. Not to mention the constant zaps each time I touch a doorknob, kiss Jay, or hug Rasta.

What should be a beautiful panorama of frozen crystals and sparkling white ground remains brown. The past several winters have lacked the heavy snow cover I recall from my childhood. I prefer trudging through and shoveling several feet of snow to exposed, frigid temperatures. Without a thick blanket of snow, frost descends deeper into the ground. I remember my mom's pipes freezing a couple of snow-deprived winters ago. A thick blanket of snow would have buffered the colder temperatures and provided some protection. Snow also serves to insulate perennial plants and the mulch-covered garlic bulbs I planted back in late October. Snow cover helps with the up and down variation of temperatures we might experience. It acts as additional cover for my strawberry plants, beyond the layer of leaves that protects them. The *Farmer's Almanac* describes how those fluctuations can damage perennial roots, like our aronia and blackberry bushes. Soil heaving is caused by the exposure of bare ground to sun and warmer temperatures.

I am starting to feel that growing anxiety I have felt in previous years as we experience another brown winter. *Waniyetu* is the time when snow lives—at least it is supposed to. At a latitude of 45 degrees, approximately halfway between the equator and the North Pole, our area ought to experience all four seasons. Yet, it seems as though climate change is increasing temperatures and growing seasons, giving way to drier conditions and erratic weather patterns. Overall, we had frequent drought conditions during this past growing season, and now with little snow, I wonder how the upcoming time of changing seasons will be.

In March, we typically experience heavy wet snows that melt quickly. This type of snow serves as a seed propagator. The prairie grasses and flowers that cover patches on our lands and line the ditches in front of our home have long dropped their seed. Scientists call this process stratification, where the snow pushes seeds farther down into the ground, ensuring reproduction. I wonder if there will be a time where I won't be able to brush my hands across the little bluestem grass or gaze at blazing star flowers. Reflecting on the importance of snow for our climate has me thinking about the winters of my childhood. Snow memories surface. I'm transported to the year we moved from the suburbs to the farm, where I spent most of my childhood. My dad had proudly shared more than once that "we bought our place sight unseen." I was seven years old that first winter, exploring the lands bundled up in hat, scarf, and mittens Mom had knitted. My brother and I loved making snow forts from the big snow piles dad created with his tractor and plow. There was so much snow to trudge through. One time my plastic camel-colored boots that zipped up along the inside of my legs got stuck in the snow ditch. My brother, two years younger, went to fetch Ma to rescue me from the deep snow. Frustrated and angry, as moms can get when they cannot solve a problem you created, she instructed me to just pull my foot out. As I did, my sock stayed in the boot, but that did not stop my mom from hollering, "Run to the house!" I ran as fast as I could up the ditch and across the yard, through the front porch, and into our wood-heated home. I recall this ditch and several more that Mom would obsessively mow down into a lawn beyond necessary. I wonder what indigenous grasses and flowers would have grown within the deep ditches that surrounded our family farm, in what is called the deciduous or Big Woods region. Today, the ditches that line my front lawn overlooking the river valley are reseeded with prairie grasses and flowers that will never be mowed. Yet, we need those big snows. What is the future of the prairie grasses and flowers I so love?

OFFERS STORY AND CONNECTION

I've got my head in the meat freezer as I pull out some beef bones the tribe gave us through the pantry program developed during the pandemic. I also grab a package of venison from dad's yearly hunt. Nearing eighty, he continues to hunt deer with my brother, just two miles from the farmplace where I grew up. Although recently, I heard him say he might not be up to all the work it takes for him to stay in his hunting camper during the nine days of open firearm season. He may just hunt at his relocated home. I say relocated because my dad loved being on the farm in the Big Woods region, but my mom longed to return to her homelands at Pejuhutazizi. And so, several years ago, we talked my dad into leaving the farm and coming west to the prairie along the Mni Sota River. He didn't like the move, not one bit. But eventually they found a country home with a few acres, and it is just a few miles from our place. Dad has his garden, cuts wood for heating their home, and has built a shop for tinkering on motors. I am grateful to have them nearby. Plus, the tribe takes good care of Mom as an elder member.

I moved over to the vegetable and fruit freezer. Yes, I have more than one freezer and I keep the meat separate, just for organization's sake. I wanted to try out the little cabbageheads I grew for the first time, including them in my vegetable soup. I grabbed one of the bags of cabbages, as well as green beans, carrots, and a bag of tomato sauce. I put all of these in the fridge to thaw for making soup the next day.

In the morning, I take out my big red enamel pot. It was an expensive purchase at the time, but a worthwhile investment for anyone who makes as much soup as I do. I pour a small amount of vegetable oil in the pot to heat it up. I am disappointed in the soupbones from the pantry program. Was the butcher a new apprentice and didn't know any better? Or did they know better but didn't care—after all, it was just for us Indians? I sigh and hope it is the former while I slice off the blue-tinted thick band of tendon around the soup cut. Then I plop the soupbones into the heated pot. I move on to the select meat, a package of venison. OMG! It cuts like butter, and I now see this is the backstrap—the tenderloin. Eek! I hold a brief moment of regret in my breath and wonder if the best cut of the deer is wasted on soup. I should have fried these up with onions! Gratitude replaces my short-lived regret as I think of Dad and brother Rob sitting for days in towering deer stands near my childhood home.

After adding the chunks of meat, I sprinkle a few dashes of Worcestershire sauce on the meat and then head to the laundry room and grab some garlic and three small red and yellow onions. I make note that there are only a half dozen remaining and frown at the thought of buying onions. I quickly chop up the onion first and throw it in with the now semi-browned meat and soupbone mixture, stirring it a bit. I add chopped celery and two cloves of finely chopped garlic, and I sprinkle in salt and pepper. I dash downstairs to my makeshift pantry, a space below the steps. I select two giant oddly shaped German Butterball potatoes. Challenged with cleaning and peeling these due to the bulbous outgrowths, I suspect their odd shapes are likely due to this past year's drought. We were careful to provide adequate room during planting and mounding as the plants grew. While we watered throughout the dry spells, I remember that plants do know the difference between rain and well water. Despite their shape, they will taste fine.

After adding the diced potatoes, I pour some water over the mix. *Chshhhh*—the meat seems to hiss in gratitude for the liquid, which prevents the meat from burning. The soup will require a lot more liquid and so I look in the fridge and pull out a half-filled pint of leftover salsa and add that. I fill the jar with water and swish it around so that it grabs the remaining bits of tomato and pepper and add that too. A jar of salsa adds such great flavor to any soup.

Salsa making is a daylong endeavor for us. I always put Jay in charge of chopping the jalapeños and hot peppers—because of his years in construction, his hands and fingers seem to be immune to the heat. Mom bought me an onion chopper years ago, and it saves the amount of time our eyes and noses run when we cut onions. And the featured ingredient is our delicious heirloom tomatoes! We had a bumper crop this past year from the twenty plants we started from seed. My senses float briefly on the memories in the jungle of plants—the plant's furry leaves that stick to my clothes, their tiny hairs that hold moisture; the distinct earthy smell of tomato plants that I love and that also serves to deter pests. I recall the frustration I felt when I tried to prop up plants that towered above me without breaking their stems. This vegetable, or rather fruit, is essential to so many meals, whether it's the base—for spaghetti—or an enhancer, as in vegetable soup. Okay, back to the soup making.

Next, I throw in a bag each of green beans and chopped carrots. The harvest of the green beans and carrots was minimal this past year. While the green bean plants started out beautifully, cucumber beetles attacked them. This is an insect I have never had to deal with—and they were relentless. Still, the two rows produced enough to freeze around two dozen bags. The carrot harvest, too, was dwarfed in comparison to previous years. I pulled them earlier than usual, tired of dragging the garden hose to the raised beds I grew them in. Carrots remain one of my favorite things to harvest. There is just something enticing about digging your hands in the soil, uncovering the orange taproots with your fingernails caked in packed dirt. After gathering them together, I stand over the raised bed and pull the carrot tops off and leave them in the bed. Isn't this regeneration—growing something that supports the renewal and restoration of the soils I will plant in again? I smile now remembering I still have a small batch of fresh whole carrots in the refrigerator—delighted they can last so long.

Now for those baby cabbageheads. I begin to chop them up, but their somewhat rubbery texture makes it challenging. So, I decide it will be okay to add the larger pieces. The heads are much smaller than the large cabbageheads my dad has grown in previous years. Dad usually grows the cabbage, along with cucumbers and dill. This year Mom shared that he could not find any starters and so I bought eight plants, intending to give him four. I was grateful to have found them at a local school's Future Farmers of America greenhouse, a student-led social enterprise I was happy to support. Yet, upon my return, my dad had located and purchased his own plants. Thus, I ended up planting all eight plants in my beds. I had never planted cabbage before, and it was challenging in a drought. I pulled the smaller heads when I started to notice something was eating them but left the root and outer leaves intact. Later in the season, they started growing mini heads, like Brussel sprouts. I ended up giving those to Dad as it turned out his cabbage did not survive. Unfortunately, during droughts, insects tend to show up in hoards.

I open a bag plumb full of thawed-out tomato sauce. Toward the end of the tomato season, I run a batch of tomatoes through the Sauce Master Food Strainer. It is the same process when we make tomato soup. The helpful device was gifted from Mom and Dad one Christmas. It works so slick when we get together to make batches of tomato soup to preserve. At the end of the tomato-growing season and long after you've canned everything you can think of, I then turn to freezing chopped tomatoes. If I have a lot, I will run them through the strainer for tomato juice. Then I just pour the juice into quart bags and freeze them. In the past, I have also canned the juice, but this is just as good and less work. Adding tomato juice to soup makes it even more flavorful.

I stir my pot now, looking to see what else I should add. I open the small freezer under the refrigerator and look around. Oooh, peas and corn. The dried corn in the freezer is not mine but was gifted from a friend. I am not sure where it is from, but it seems to be dehydrated and the kernels are bigger than what I am used to. Later, I tasted some and noticed they are not as sweet as mine, and they didn't quite puff up the way they should. I have never dehydrated my corn but dry it in the sun, which I think makes all the difference. I pour about a half of cup of peas in and notice that I only have about one cup remaining. I did not plant the usual big, long row of peas along a fence this past year. I have done this in previous years and was able to freeze at least two gallon bags of shelled peas, more than Jay and I can eat in a year. But now I realize that the small amount I planted this year was not enough. Note to self: Plant a half row of peas next year.

I top the soup off with some of my own dried chives and pars-ley, I add more water, stir, and bring it to a simmer. I cover the pot and let it cook for some time, perhaps a couple of hours, stirring occasionally, before turning the heat down to make sure it doesn't burn. The soup smells divine. I move it to the back burner on low until supper time.

That evening, Jay says, "Best soup ever." I smile, thinking he says that every time I make soup. I reflect on the cooking prepa-ration, noticing that I have a lot of experiential memories with most of the ingredients. Yet, the beef bones provided by the tribe, purchased through a locker, fail to illicit any memory or past sen-sory experience. While I know that the ingredients grown from my garden or even the tenderloins from Dad's successful hunt provide top nutrients and flavor, I realize they also connect me to land and remind me of the relationships we hold with our plant and animal relatives. This is what brings deep gratitude to the cooking process and the anticipation of a good meal.

❖   ❖   ❖   ❖

Venison Vegetable Stew

1 tablespoon vegetable oil
1–2 soupbones
2 pounds venison roast

recipe continued ▶

1 tablespoon Worcestershire sauce
1 onion, chopped
2–3 stalks celery, chopped
2–3 cloves garlic, chopped
1½ cups chopped cabbage
1 cup green beans
1 cup sliced carrots
2 small potatoes, cubed
2 cups tomato sauce
salt and pepper
½ cup peas
½ cup corn
½ jar salsa
1 tablespoon dried chives
1 teaspoon parsley

Heat oil in Dutch oven or soup pot. Add soupbones. Chop roast into bite-size chunks and add to pot. Sprinkle Worcestershire sauce over meat. Add onions and celery, and when they are translucent, add garlic. Add remaining ingredients. Add water to desired level and consistency. Season. Bring to a boil, turn down heat and simmer until vegetables are fork tender. Turn heat down to low until ready to serve.

PROVIDES INTIMACY AND SOLITUDE

In my office, I have a picture framed with a quotation and an image in the background of Charles Eastman sitting outside in solitude. The Dakota scholar from generations ago speaks to the importance of silence in keeping balance: "With silence comes the character of self-control, courage, and reverence." I am thinking on his words as I wake to the shortest day and longest night of the year. Emerging from my bed after some hip and leg stretches, eyes half-closed, I shuffle my feet to the window. I open each of the three blinds, which emit only darkness because there is no light at this time of the morning and during this time of year. I peer out and look slightly to the right. In the southeast skies I see

Winter solstice backyard.

the morning star and acknowledge gratitude for the day. My gratitudes include the *Dakota Wicohaŋ* family, as I look forward to the evening's holiday party with them; having slept well last night; and the upcoming life changes this new year will bring.

After going through my morning routine, I sit down for my morning coffee at my laptop. I smile to myself, appreciating the semi-habit of writing I've maintained. I peer out the front window, making note of how much the eastern sunrise has moved toward the south. I recall the early-summer mornings on the porch with coffee just a few months ago. During that time, the sun poked through the maple that sits toward the north end of our front yard. Either season, whether from our front porch or looking out the frigid window, the sunrises we experience shine magnificently on the bluff overlooking the prairie. The orange, pink, and peach-colored bursts center and ground me as one small piece of stardust in all of creation.

These mornings when I have been able to keep the television turned off (because Jay loves the sound of television) and bask in the silence, my days feel hopeful and deliberate. With the turning of increased light, my body, mind, and spirit will soon shift into planning mode. But for today, the solstice reminds me to stay present, observant, and silent.

❖   ❖   ❖   ❖

Tomato Soup, canned

12–14 quarts juice from fresh tomatoes
1 large sweet pepper
6 small onions
6–8 celery stalks
4 cups chopped carrots
1 scant cup sugar
½ cup butter
¼ cup canning salt
1 cup flour

Clean and quarter ripe tomatoes, removing stems. Juice tomatoes until at least 12–14 quarts are achieved. We use a Sauce Master to juice the tomatoes, in the process filtering skins and seeds. Pour juice into a nonstick 16-quart soup pot. Chop vegetables and add to the tomato juice. Cook and bring to a simmer, stirring and mashing vegetables to extract more juice from them. Once vegetables are soft, using a hand strainer, remove vegetables. My parents like their soup to incorporate the vegetables (like V-8) and will blend the vegetables smooth. Add sugar and cook for another 5 minutes. Cream together butter, salt, and flour. Drop this creamed mixture into soup and continue to blend and stir until creamy, cooking for another 10 minutes. I use an extra-long handheld blender. Pour into hot sterilized quart or pint jars, add a few drops of commercially bottled lemon juice, and seal. Process the jars in a hot water bath for 15 minutes. This soup is so good, far beyond Campbell's condensed tomato soup. This recipe is adapted from the Gethsemane Church cookbook from 1977 (I added clarity to terms from the original recipe, such as "peck" and a "bunch"). A simple meal of tomato soup and a grilled cheese sandwich brings comfort during the solstice season. I find solace by walking downstairs to our pantry and pulling out a pint of comfort.

RESTORATIVE

I finally was motivated and interested in trekking outside on the trails. Considering myself a "hardy" girl, I have always enjoyed bundling up and hiking the lands, observing the dormancy and beauty that abounds. I don't know if it's from getting older, perhaps it's the thought of cold creeping into my bones and aching joints, but going outside has not appealed to me this winter—until now. So I am drawn to leave the comfortable seventy-degree enclosure to venture into the five-below-zero weather to connect with our sleeping mother.

Rasta-girl, our canine, eagerly joins me. She's jumping up and down as I descend the stairs and is nipping at the walking sticks that provide support for my bone-on-bone knee joints. Walking east and toward the trailhead, I can feel the tiny hairs in my nose freeze together as I inhale the frigid air. On the trail and listening acutely now, I begin trekking down its curvy descent into the woods.

There is something about winter landscapes that evokes attentiveness. Every sound seems sharper. The crunch of my boots on the snow, my steady breath, and the swish of my coat with each step are acutely heard. Rasta is now out of sight, and I call for her to wait up. We haven't taken her down the trails since she took down a doe in mid-November. Jay was barely able to pull her off as her teeth sunk into its hindquarter. She is, after all, a Rottweiler Lab. He dragged Rasta's eighty pounds up to the house, then returned with his gun in case he had to put the deer down. But she was nowhere to be found—both of us were relieved and disappointed at the same time. (Have I told you I love venison?)

I continue walking and the dog finally gallops past me. She stops, sniffs the air, and then scoops up snow in her mouth. She seems to be smiling now, so happy to be playing, free of the collar that keeps her within a hundred-foot perimeter. I notice a bird's nest full of snow and think about the birds that have migrated south. I take in the numerous rabbit tracks meandering in and off the trail into thickets and brush.

Winter cedar branch on the trail.

Deeper now into the woods, I choose the pathway that rolls into a picturesque scene with cedar boughs bent down from the weight of snow and ice. I hear sounds of pheasant wings, likely being flushed out by Rasta. I silently pray they make it to a tree branch. I hear another one as I opt for a right turn out of the woods and onto a trail that circles around the prairie grasses. Rasta now joins me at a slower pace, and I can see her breath with each pant. I take note of the snow art along the trail. Just like when we make snow angels, the prairie grass tips make snow arches from moving back and forth in the wind.

Nearing the end of our trail now, I walk alongside the row of lilacs and the many different varieties we planted. Lilacs or *Syringa* are a part of the olive tree family and native to eastern Europe. To bloom in the spring, they need cold weather like our *Mni Sota* winters to shift into dormancy. I carry that thought with me as I call Rasta, now making my way back toward the house. She looks at me as if to question "Already? We're having so much fun!" I concede but only for a short time, just long enough to shovel snow from the deck before moving back indoors to thaw out. I pull the ingredients for a spicy black bean soup that will warm my innards and clear sinus congestion.

Gazing out the kitchen window, I reflect on the sleeping lilacs and what the acupuncturist had told me during my last session. That our bodies, too, need time to rest and restore so that we can have the energy in the spring for all that needs to be done. His words provided me the permission I needed to curl up on the couch, be dormant for the day, and wait for that soup to be ready.

✦   ✦   ✦   ✦

Spicy Black Bean Soup

2 cups dried black beans, cooked
2 teaspoons olive oil
1 cup chopped green peppers
1 onion, chopped
salt and pepper
4 cloves garlic, minced
2 chicken breasts, cut in bite-size pieces
1 quart frozen chopped tomatoes
1 cup frozen sweet corn
1 quart tomato sauce
2 teaspoons cumin
½ cup green chili sauce
4 ounces cream cheese or sour cream
2 teaspoons dried cilantro

Soak beans overnight. Rinse and cook beans until tender. I prefer Hopi Black Turtle Beans as they cook up quickly; I have even cooked them without soaking. Mandan Black Beans take a bit longer to cook and benefit from overnight soaking. In a Dutch oven or soup pot, add oil and heat on medium heat. Add chopped green peppers and onion, and season with salt and pepper. When onions are nearly translucent, add minced garlic and stir. Add chicken pieces to the pot. If desired, season chicken with southwestern seasoning. Next, add cooked beans, chopped tomatoes, corn, tomato sauce, and cumin. If you don't have frozen chopped tomatoes, substitute canned tomatoes or a jar of salsa. Bring to a simmer and add green chili sauce (you can add more, depending on desired spice level). On a low simmer, cook for 45 minutes. Keep warm and stir in cream cheese or sour cream before serving and top with sliced jalapeños. I serve this with corn muffins made with chopped jalapeños and shredded cheddar cheese.

SYNCHRONIZING

The light is coming, although I have yet to sense, notice, or feel it. We are supposedly gaining light, but it is still pitch dark as we drink our morning coffee. What started out as gaining a few additional seconds of light post–winter solstice is now up to a minute. Today we will have nearly nine hours of daylight and a month from now—ten hours. By mid-March, the rising sun will wake me instead of Rasta's barking and her howling at the coyotes. But then, of course, the man-made clock-changing regimen called daylight savings time will require me to spring out of bed before sunrise again. I will say, though, that being up before the sun allows me to gaze out the window and watch the horizon's amazing change of colors from dark orange, bright pink, peach, and finally to yellow.

These shifts slowly call me out of the winter slumber. One of the first activities out of our seasonal hibernation is to assess the food stock. This helps me consider what I need to plant and what I ought to take a break from. Some things, despite being stocked

Winter backyard.

up, will not be given a reprieve. For example, I have plenty of dried fruit, jams, and jellies, but the berries, apples, and pears are perennials. They will have to be harvested regardless. However, my mind and body are not quite ready to transition to planning mode, and I revert to rest mode. There is still time for planning—plenty of time.

✦   ✦   ✦   ✦

Honey Thyme Apples and Egg Breakfast

1 apple
2 teaspoons honey
1 teaspoon dried thyme
4 slices Canadian bacon, chopped
6–8 eggs
3 ounces white cheddar cheese
1–2 teaspoons olive oil

This is a fantastic savory dish, and I still have Honeycrisp and Golden Delicious apples stored from this past season's harvest. Add olive oil to a cast iron pan. While the oil is heating, thinly slice the apple. Add to the hot pan, drizzle with locally sourced honey, and add dried thyme (mine is from my garden!). Once some of the apples are lightly browned, toss and stir. Add Canadian bacon. Remove from heat. Whisk locally sourced eggs and add small chunks of white cheddar or some other hard, savory cheese. Pour over apples and put the cast iron pan in a 350-degree oven. Bake for 20 minutes. I served this for my son Tanner this winter with sliced toast and a glass of our apple cider. I was tickled when he curiously asked, "Mmmm, what's in this?"

A QUALITY OF LIFE

Waŋna waniyetu wikcemna zaptaŋ sam matopa. Now I am fifty-four winters. I lie in bed, telling myself to sleep in as long as I like, without guilt. While lying there, not really sleeping but thinking about what I wanted to do today, I reflect on my age and the fact that I am likely over halfway there. *Where is there?* I wonder.

Okay, not today. But my grandma came to my mind. She lived to be nearly ninety-seven years old, and Grandpa ninety-five. But then I thought of my dad's side: Grandma Meta, who lived to sixty-four, and my dad's dad, fifty-nine. Eek! But then my dad is outliving both his parents. He is active, still cutting wood to heat his home, working on classic cars, and each season he grows cucumbers, dill, onions, carrots, cabbage, and tomatoes in his garden. My maternal grandparents gardened, too, far into their later years. Mom told of the mounds of potatoes they planted and piled up in the basement each year. Even after my grandpa passed away and Grandma was more homebound, she still had her indoor plants and outdoor perennials to admire. My great-grandparents on my dad's side were subsistence farmers and have memories of Great-Grandma Emma, who lived a long life. And my stepgrandpa Harvey outlived my grandma by many years, and he always had a garden, fished, and hunted. I cannot help but believe that gardening has had a positive impact on life expectancies or at least on the quality of life. The nerd in me has to do the research. And yes of course it does!

Several studies suggest gardening has positive impacts on quality of life. For example, people suffering from dementia and Alzheimer's report feeling less agitated in garden settings. I learned that Okinawa has the highest number of centenarians. I used to tease my grandma that she would live to be a centenarian, especially when she would ask morbid questions, like "Why is it taking so long?" My guess was that she was lonesome for Grandpa. In Okinawa, it appears there is a link between the high number of centenarians and having gardens, but additionally, they take their produce to local markets. The social connectivity in sharing what they grow also provides a purpose in their lives. There are a significant number of studies demonstrating the benefits of nature bathing, including reduced blood pressure and anxiety and increased happiness. In fact, many health practitioners are now prescribing these types of connections with nature for health-related issues. Further, gardeners often grow the vegetables they will eat, thus increasing the amount and quality of fresh fruits, vegetables, and legumes in their diets, which we all know contribute to improved health. The literature I read only affirms what I intuitively know: overall, I will experience increased health and well-being as I engage in the ceremony of gardening.

Still, I recently made a commitment to take a year off from gardening, to let the soil rest and to allow myself the freedom to travel. And now I wonder about what will be lost if I do that. I consider the possibility of balancing, *both/and.* How could I let the soil rest, do some traveling, and still experience and gain the benefits of nurturing plants, eating homegrown healthy fruits and vegetables, and bring people together for those important social connections? I think about my grandma and how she loved to admire her azalea tree and lilac bushes outside. From her walker, she would point to her sedums and bleeding hearts in the spring poking through the ground. I dug up some of those sedums after she passed away and planted them in my back yard and have watched them flourish and spread even more. Tears well up and a smile spreads across my face. I am in awe that my grandma is still teaching me, passing on life lessons through her spirit and memory. It is in that moment that I decide part of this year's planning process will include nurturing outdoor perennials and memory spaces throughout our yard. That in addition to assessing what I *really need* to grow in our big vegetable garden (meaning planting less), I will include tending to the ecosystem that surrounds our sanctuary, the land we call home. Here's to an abundant fifty-fourth year!

ADAPTABLE

I am assessing my bean stock selection displayed on my kitchen counter. I am nearly out of kidney, Hopi Black Turtle, and Bumble Bee beans. But I have the Cherokee Red Peanut beans, which are great for chili, the Mandan Black beans, which take longer to cook than the Hopis, and a lot of alternative beans for soup, like Arikara Yellow, Lina Sisco Bird Egg. I really do not need to grow beans this coming year—as tempting as it is. This is the process I will need to follow. Go through my storage and decide what I absolutely need to plant—keeping in mind that it will be a minimal vegetable garden with my heart set on supporting the ecosystem that supports my gardening. Not to mention it supports me and is the right thing to do.

After evaluating the beans, I decided I should make some hummus. I chose the Brown Tepary beans from the Tohono O'odham Nation. The *Wepegi Bawi*, in their language, is a small, nutty-flavored bean and is perfect for making hummus. This bean is heat and drought resistant, having been nurtured in the Sonoran Desert. The Tohono O'odham share that *Wepegi Bawi* is high in protein and is very low (29) on the glycemic index, making this a diabetic-friendly food. According to *The Impact of Food Assistance Programs on the Tohono O'odham Food System: An Analysis and Recommendations,* a report published through the Center for World Indigenous Studies, the people of the Tohono O'odham Nation have more than a 50 percent rate of diabetes.

Stored beans.

This is the highest rate in the world. I recognize this as a result of colonialism, loss of land, language, and lifeways. Our people, too, suffer from high rates of diabetes, just like many other Indigenous peoples in the United States. I remember Grandma was diabetic and Mom too is afflicted, as are others in our family and community.

Several years ago I found an advertisement in the *Native Foods* magazine for their Tepary beans. It piqued my interest and so I bought both the White and Brown Tepary beans. They arrived in cute brown paper sacks with directions on how to cook them. I kept a small handful of each and planted them the following year. They grew nicely in our somewhat dense clay soil, despite being in a completely different climate. I have planted them ever since, as their flavor is outstanding. Making hummus is one of the ways I like to prepare these beans. In sharing, I've been asked many times for the recipe. I am quite sure I make it differently each time, but here is a description of the most recent version of hummus I made.

Soak about a half cup of dried Tepary beans overnight. Rinse thoroughly and cook the beans. For such a small bean, they require a bit more time to cook. So be sure to use enough water or watch them closely and add more water as needed. Once they are fully cooked, strain the water from the cooked beans. Put the beans in a food processor. Add a can of chickpeas (garbanzo) beans. This is a bean I have yet to grow. After roasting garlic cloves with a little olive oil in the oven, add them to the processor. I like garlic, so I use four or five cloves. Add three tablespoons or more of tahini. Add the juice of half a lemon. I have also pulled out some sun-dried tomatoes from the freezer and added about half a cup of those. Season to taste, including salt, pepper, dried oregano, and hot pepper seasoning. I keep on hand a variety of dehydrated hot peppers that are ground to a pulp. Then blend while adding olive oil and a bit of water for a smooth consistency. Making hummus is a trial, taste test, and adjust type of process. I have never had a bad-tasting hummus. It just requires some creativity and adjustments.

Hummus

1 cup cooked Tepary beans
1 can chickpeas, strained
4 cloves garlic
½ cup sun-dried tomatoes
3–4 tablespoons tahini
½ lemon
3–4 tablespoons olive oil
seasonings
water, as needed

Cook Tepary beans in boiling water, strain when fully cooked. In an oven preheated to 325 degrees, roast garlic tossed with a small amount of olive oil until tender in a small, covered pot. In food processor, pulse the beans and chickpeas. Add garlic, tomatoes, and tahini. Squeeze juice from half a lemon. While pulsing, drizzle in the olive oil. Add seasonings to taste, pulsing in between and tasting. Add a bit of water if smoother consistency is desired. Seasonings can include salt, pepper, dried oregano, cumin. I have also used a combination of paprika, chili powder, and dried hot pepper. The seasonings will enhance over time.

Chili

2 cups dried kidney beans
1 tablespoon olive oil
4 stalks celery, chopped
1 onion, chopped
1 pound buffalo burger
2 pints salsa
1 quart tomato sauce
water, as needed
chili seasoning to taste

Soak beans overnight. Rinse beans and cook until tender. Add oil in Dutch oven or soup pot on medium heat. Add chopped celery and onion and cook for a few minutes. Add burger and cook through. Add salsa, tomato sauce, and water. Add chili seasoning as desired. I also like to add some hot pepper powder for more kick. Let simmer for at least an hour. I have used other beans besides kidney, including Hidatsa Red and Cherokee Red Peanut beans. Sometimes I will cook a half cup of a dried butter bean type, like Scarlet Runner or Christmas Lima bean. Just be sure to cook these beans separately from the others as they take a longer time to cook.

COMING HOME

We are back home. Home to where Rasta-girl greets us, her boxy girth nearly knocking us over. We are welcomed by all the creature comforts we have thoughtfully arranged throughout the house, creating a sanctuary we crave when absent. Our home is where all three boys will return for comfort food and common conversation. It is near to my parents, who feel secure knowing we are a ten-minute drive away. Our space is also home to many outdoor relatives—cardinals, blue jays, finches, and chickadees that congregate at the bird feeders. Tommy and Tippy, our mousers, test their prowess with the birds. The *waŋbdi* (eagle) and *cetaŋ* (hawk) circle for the cats. The maples, cedars, and oaks surround our space. And the sounds of life across our lands and in the waters wrap our refuge. Thirteen days is the longest time either of us has been away from all that we call home. These are the comforts we so longed for.

No. The answer is no. Jay and I wondered if we could migrate south for warmer weather in exchange for *Mni Sota* winters, like the life of our snowbird friends. So, as a test we extended our annual weeklong Florida trip by another week. "This is not a vacation," I told Jay as I unpacked my work laptop. That might have been true for me, but Jay spent his days golfing with his Anishinaabe friend Tom and strolling the beach. Mine were the activities of work life—Zoom calls, calendars, and to-dos all neatly tucked within a slim sixteen-inch metal rectangle with attached cords. I did get to enjoy Tuesday movie nights with half-price theater popcorn. We also spent a Saturday afternoon at the Marine Laboratory and Aquarium—a visual festival of fish, manatees, octopuses, and jellyfish. Weather-dependent mornings included meditative walks to the beach just across the street, as we gathered shells and listened to the surfs and sprays of the gulf. There was a bountiful variety of restaurants and meals, unlike our rural spaces back home. Despite all that was available and lovely, I longed for the mundane routines of home.

Upon our return home and a good night's sleep in my own bed, I make a nourishing and hearty breakfast of wild rice, nuts, and blueberries, sweetened by our own maple syrup. After unpacking, I prepare the upcoming evening meal. I fill a crockpot full of beef chunks, carrots, onions, and golden mushroom soup for a gravy mix. Later I pair the main dish with mashed potatoes and green beans. This simple meal, most of its ingredients nurtured and gathered right outside our abode, provides nourishment and satiates us, welcoming us back to Dakota homelands.

❖   ❖   ❖   ❖

Haȟaŋna Psiŋ

wild rice
milk or cream
hazelnuts
maple syrup
blueberries

Susan, my Anishinaabe sister friend, made a variation of this recipe for me years ago. It is a hearty breakfast! Cook up wild rice only in water (no chicken broth here). I will typically make this when I have cooked up too much wild rice and will store it in the refrigerator for breakfast a few times. Heat up the desired amount of wild rice in a bowl. Add your choice of dairy/nondairy; I prefer nonfat vanilla-flavored almond milk. Sister likes hers with cream. Stir in a little maple syrup, maybe a tablespoon. Add roasted and chopped hazelnuts, but any nut is fine. Add a handful of blueberries.

STILLNESS

I stepped out on the deck for my morning greeting to all that is. My mini sun salutation provides me opportunity to put the day's tasks into perspective. Sometimes the stars are still visible, and I recognize the infinite possibilities and experiences that lie before me. Other times, the sun in all its glorious rising causes sherbet-colored hues of melon and fuchsia to line the horizon, and joy emanates from my core. This day, in early January, was cloudy and calm. The quiet was noticeable—I did not hear even a distant car. I wondered if *all that is* were taking in this moment as well. I savored the stillness by slowly scanning my vision from east to south, taking in my surroundings, and then east to north. And then I saw her—a doe lying on the edge of the big pines, just a few steps from the edge of our garden. Her brown body caught my eye, silhouetted against the white snow and dark green trees above her. Deer are masters of observation and would typically run at the sight, sound, or smell of a threat. Yet she remained where she was. Her black gazing eyes connected briefly with mine as we took in the stillness of the morning.

APOLITICAL

The Super Bowl menu is buffalo enchiladas, sprinkled with sliced southwest chilis, and my son Mani's favorite beef-and-bean dip. To top it off, we have a lovely apricot coffee cake for dessert, in-spired and apricot-sourced by my friend Mary Jo. Jay and I couldn't wait until the evening when our boys would join us for the meal and game. Seriously, we could not wait, and indulged in a slice of the freshly baked apricot coffee cake with a cup of joe. The late lunch treat was delicious, not too sweet, and perfect with a hot caffeinated beverage. With each bite, I am thinking of Mary Jo, who provided the apricots in our good food trade this past harvest season. In addition to the giant Miami squashes she shared, she generously topped off the trade with a quart of halved apricots and a mini jelly jar of apricot slurry, compliments of her orchard.

Our friends Mary Jo and her husband, Luverne, are certified organic farmers on a 480-acre plot. They live northwest a little more than an hour's drive from us. Their multigenerational family farm was passed down through Luverne's side of the family. They raise grass-fed beef and a ton of fruits and vegetables. Mary Jo sells products that they raise from a small on-farm shop, but I suspect she gives away a large portion of her goods to family and friends. I have been one of her lucky recipients and we agreed to trade produce this past season. I already know that I want apricots to be on my wish list for future trades.

I cannot imagine the amount of work they take on each year to ensure their produce qualifies for the organic certification. Luverne, a burly guy with rough hands who meets the cliché "strong as an ox," is a warmhearted, gentle man who welcomes a good hug. During visits, he is usually outside taking care of their cattle, ensuring pasture rotation and all that goes into raising the herbivores. Mary Jo, tall with shoulder-length, graying blond hair and intense blue eyes, is a lover of the prairie. I met her at the University of Minnesota, Morris when she was the healthy eating coordinator. A registered dietitian by trade, she became an advocate for Indigenous reclamation efforts, including traditional foods. She is an avid listener who seeks understanding and finds ways to support. Before retiring, she helped Indigenous students at UMN, Morris in reclaiming gardening practices and cooking Native foods. She continues these efforts, despite being retired, as I just received an invitation to "Soups, Seeds, and Stories," an event she is hosting at her farm. She sees hope for the future in the intersection of Native students, community members, and food sovereignty efforts.

Mary Jo is a quiet fighter. She and Luverne are working to protect their crops from cross-pollination with GMO crops that dominate the landscape. Large agribusiness entities have replaced neighboring farmers and control thousands of acres of land, using planes and large ground sprayers to apply pesticides and commercial fertilizers. Mary Jo uses farm events, community education, and any opportunity that emerges to disseminate their organic farming practices and preserve the tall grass prairie ecosystem for future generations. She does this through sharing tasty foods to try to increase interest in the care of the land, air, water, and foods we humans need to live.

One of Mary Jo's other strategies is to attempt to hold people accountable to the laws protecting the interdependent relationship we have with the land, air, and water. She has reported violations that govern best practices in spraying pesticides and disposing of carcasses that have adversely affected their organic farm. She makes her reports to the Minnesota Board of Animal Health and Minnesota Department of Agriculture, and more recently she provided written testimony to the Minnesota House of Representatives Agriculture Finance and Policy Committee.

In addition to the five-year account she chronicles, the pictures also tell the story. Photographs include a not-so-decomposed turkey carcass and a bag that held ZetaGard LBT (poultry litter beetle treatment) insecticide, examples of the debris from neighboring fields blown by wind and dragged by predators across their organic farm. Another photo of prairie grass–covered lands adjacent to a wetland area shows a giant pile of something that looks like a layer of snow around the perimeter. Written on the bottom of the photograph is "turkey feathers attached to carcasses." I zoom in on the photograph of the ZetaGard bag Mary Jo emailed me. Its label lists Zetacypermethrin, Piperonyl Butoxide, and "other ingredients." After some quick research, I find that Cypermethrin is a synthetic chemical first developed in 1974, similar to an extract found in the chrysanthemum plant. A fact sheet pops up on my screen from the National Pesticide Information Center. In general, it explains that if humans handle Cypermethrin, some tingling, burning, dizziness, and itching may occur. And if the chemical is ingested (and yes, there have been human volunteers), most of it is excreted within twenty-four hours. The fact sheet also includes descriptions of experimental results from tests done on mice to determine whether Cypermethrin is a carcinogen. The tests did not show the development of cancer, only lung tumors. Therefore, it concludes, "Scientists have no data from work-related, accidental poisoning, or epidemiological studies that indicate whether or not Cypermethrin is likely to cause cancer in humans." I can read between the lines. I only have to scroll and read further to confirm it is not safe. Cypermethrin is highly toxic to fish and bees, very highly toxic to water insects, and has very low toxicity to birds. Are you smirking like me as you read the words "highly," "very highly," and "low"—the toxicity ratings? Toxic means poisonous, no matter how you rate it, and the image that comes to my mind is the skull-and-crossbones icon found on household chemicals that signifies danger.

I am a little afraid now to look up the next ingredient, Piperonyl Butoxide (PBO). Again, I choose to get my information from what would seem like a legitimate source, the National Pesticide Information Center (NPIC). The first image on their page shows a substance coming out of a spray can, and I intuitively know it is not good. PBO has been around since the 1950s and is a manmade pesticide synergist, meaning it works to increase the effectiveness of bug killers. I learn that insects, and I will assume any living thing, have enzymes that work to break down insecticides. I feel like I am becoming a scientist. What PBO does is stop those enzymes from doing their job. With PBO, it is less likely the insects will recover, in essence allowing the insecticides to work better—to kill better. I learn PBOs are in a lot of common items— flea and tick treatments for our pets, mosquito sprays, and head lice treatments. And, it is often sprayed on almonds, tomatoes, wheat, animal meat—after harvest. Wait, what?! I am grateful we grow our own tomatoes, but how do we wash PBO from wheat? NPIC shares information on many PBO studies conducted on a diversity of living beings, including not only the typical rats but also goats, dogs, laying hens, and humans. A wide range of doses and effects are described, making it a bit difficult to decipher the extent of dangerous effects. Yet the NPIC states that "PBO is low to very low in toxicity if eaten, inhaled, or touched." Again, it seems as though our bodies will break down and remove most PBO, but what does catch my attention is that it appears to affect the livers of those animals exposed to large amounts of it; for example, increasing amounts of PBO were found in the eggs of laying hens, as well as in their meat, fat, skin, and organs. Again, this chemical appears to impact our aquatic relatives, fresh- and saltwater fish, water fleas, shrimp, and amphibians.

I decide I am not a scientist. But I do not have to be one to understand that our increasing exposure to chemicals—and count them, I looked up only two examples here—cannot be good for us, or for our plant, animal, and aquatic relatives, the water, or the land. And to think that we have been exposed to these types of chemicals since at least the 1950s, across multiple generations. I wonder if we, like chickens, may be passing PBO on to our offspring. Again, I am not a scientist, but I cannot help wondering about the increasing rates of cancer, infertility, diseases, and allergies to foods. And while this may seem like an issue wrought in politics, I wonder how protecting the necessities we all must have to live can turn into partisan battles.

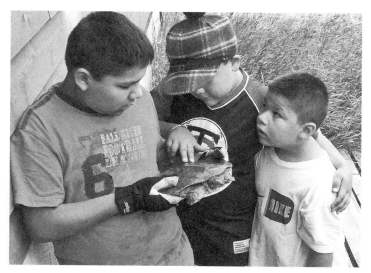

Caske, Hepaŋna, Hepi—my three boys when they were younger, with a turtle they found.

Mary Jo sent me the link to her testimony and shared, "I needed to get it out there in public to see if I can stir anyone to care about this abuse of land and water that continues to happen. Maybe others will tell their stories? Who knows? Who will care?" That is a good question, who will care? I care. And not just because I enjoy eating the big, beautiful orange squash, apricots, giant heirloom watermelons, and grass-fed beef they raise—but because wetlands on their farm flow into the Chippewa River, then into the Minnesota and Mississippi Rivers. These are the same waters that flow near our home and sanctuary. She rightfully exclaims, "This is not just our problem way out somewhere in western Minnesota—this affects all of us." How are you connected to these bodies of water and ultimately to the wetlands nestled in the prairie potholes in Pope County? More important—do you care?

✦   ✦   ✦   ✦

Apricot Coffee Cake (inspired by Mary Jo)

2 cups flour
3 teaspoons baking powder
½ teaspoon baking soda
¼ teaspoon salt
½ cup chopped apricots
2 eggs
1 cup buttermilk
½ cup sugar
¼ cup butter, melted
apricot slurry (optional)

Mix flour, baking powder, baking soda, and salt. Stir in chopped apricots. I used halved frozen apricots, but I imagine dried or fresh would work as well. In a separate bowl, mix eggs, buttermilk, sugar, and butter. Stir into flour mixture. Pour combined mixture into a 9-inch round lightly greased cake pan. Top with a bit of apricot slurry and swirl into cake mix. Sprinkle on ¼ cup chopped walnuts and cinnamon sugar mix. Bake at 350 for 35 minutes.

Mary Jo shared a little jar of apricot slurry, which is mashed apricot, making it a thick liquid with small bits of apricot.

Cake, is it healthy? Probably not, but if I am going to eat cake (and I do), I try my best to incorporate healthier adaptations. For example, we buy locally grown eggs from the neighbor down the road, whose chickens have the run of their yard, pecking away at the prairie bugs, and we incorporate homegrown fruits like these lovely apricots from our friend Mary Jo.

✦   ✦   ✦   ✦

Mani's Favorite Dip

1 pound burger
1 large onion, chopped
2 cloves of garlic, minced
1½ cups cooked Black Turtle beans
2 pints homemade salsa
2–3 jalapeños, chopped
12–16 ounces cheese
hot pepper spices

Brown the burger. We usually use buffalo, but venison, beef, or turkey is fine. Then add onion and garlic. Add the cooked beans, salsa, and jalapeños. Add spices to desired hotness. Then add a good melting cheese or cheese product. Serve with your choice of tortilla chips. One of the great things about this dip is that it is hearty enough for a meal.

A REPEATED BEHAVIOR

It is that time of the year. After the long winter rest and a few pounds heavier, I pull out the orange and brown woven basket gifted by my mother-in-law. It is overflowing with bags of various seeds. Each year before spring but after months of what people might call cabin fever, I get the itch. Tired of subzero temperatures and being cooped up indoors, I've shifted from dreaming to planning. I dump out the bags of seeds to find last year's garden map. It is imperative that I keep track of what and where I planted so that I can ensure crop rotation to avoid nutrient depletion in the soil. Along with the assessment from the pantry and freezer, I begin to list what I want to plant. On a new sheet of paper, I sketch out what and where I will plant in the coming season, while cross-referencing the wish list and last year's garden map. This year, since I will be planting less, I have decided not to work the areas where last year's plants are covered with leaves, newspaper, and grass clippings. That leaves very little space for planting. My list is fairly short, though: carrots, green beans, and onions, as we've eaten up last year's harvest. This is the time I also make a list of any seeds I may need to purchase. While most of what I plant is done through the seeds I have saved from the previous harvest, there are some plants whose seeds I have yet to practice saving. For example, seeds for spinach, lettuce, and greens I typically purchase. However, lettuce and various greens have been reseeding themselves in one of the beds because I have left the plants to grow long after prime picking. I have not had that luck with spinach. I have also yet to practice seed saving with tomatoes. Because there are different varieties I grow each year, it takes four to five years for me to use up a packet of seeds. Perhaps this year, I will try.

Looking through my seed basket, I locate the green bean seeds and find it interesting that they are just plain brown in color and not colorful like the dried beans. I am out of carrot seed, which I also purchase as needed. I cannot get myself to leave the carrots in the ground long enough to go to seed. So, this, too, I write down to purchase. Despite the fact that I won't need many seeds for this coming gardening season, I enjoy pulling out all the seeds and admire the potential of each one. I keep them somewhat organized. There is the bean bag, full of well over a dozen smaller bags containing varieties of beans. I have a corn bag with Dakota popcorn, three different years of *wamnaheza* (Indian corn), and several other traditional corn seed that people have gifted me. I would like to grow them but haven't had the heart yet to vary the alternating years of Dakota popcorn and *wamnaheza*. I have a *wamnu* bag full of the seeds of several varieties of squash, pumpkins, and melons. I frown now thinking about them. The annual battle with squash bugs, squash borers, and the more recent cucumber beetles caused me to forgo planting them—at least for a few years. Perhaps the absence of delectable fruits will cause them to move out and find some other place to take up home. I put the bag of seed down, resolute in my commitment not to plant them for a few years. At least in my garden—I could convince my boys to plant them in their yards. I look at the big bag of marigold seed. The big clumps of dried flowers containing their long black-and-white-tipped seed include several varieties. In another bag there are varieties of sunflowers, herbs, and packages of zinnia seeds. Clipped together are several varieties of tomato seed packets and another of peppers. Many of the pepper seeds are those that I easily saved from harvested peppers, including jalapeños, paprika, bells, and the chilis from the southwest. I sigh putting back all the seeds, knowing that I will be planning for just a few rows of this and that. Besides, there are still plenty of perennials in the garden that will need to be tended to. And in just twelve months from now, I will once again be able to put dreams to sketch and plan out yet another season of gardening.

❖   ❖   ❖   ❖

Chipotle Crockpot Beans

2 cups dried beans
BBQ pork loin, cooked and shredded
1 cup chopped green peppers
1 large onion, chopped
1–2 chipotles, chopped
3 cloves garlic, minced
pepper to taste
1 bottle of BBQ sauce

Select one or two varieties of dried beans that hold up well in heat (e.g., Good Mother Stallard, contender, Lina Sisco's Bird Egg beans). Soak beans in water overnight. Next morning, strain beans. Cook beans until tender but still intact. In crockpot, add beans, shredded pork, green peppers and onions, chipotles, garlic, and pepper. Add BBQ sauce; add a little bit of water to bottle, swish to gain remaining sauce, add to crockpot, and cover. Cook at 350 for an hour and turn to low until ready to eat.

FIGHTING THE GOOD FIGHT

I've got a big pot of *paśdayapi* on the stove to fuel us up on ancient nutrition *to fight the good fight.* I remember this phrase during my grandpa's funeral and understand its roots in Christianity and morality. And while I am no fighter (it's just not part of my DNA), the intended struggle is in making good choices and helping others to improve the world around us. Seems like that could include protecting relatives—like people, water, and Mother Earth.

Our fight today is against carbon pipelines, and we are battling using our words. A few weeks ago, *Icepaŋśi* Gaby (who by the way *is* a fearless fighter) called on a collective of five of us to attend a public information session on carbon dioxide pipelines proposed in our region. So, four Dakotas—Gaby, Sharon, me, and my son Hunter—and our allied Irish activist, Mary, walked into a room filled with more than two hundred farmers and landowners. Yeah, you can imagine how we drew a few stares, but familiar faces from an ally organization, Clean Up the River Environment, were also in attendance. They carefully shared their informational message and expressed concerns about the unknown effects of the planned carbon pipeline on the environment and people. Despite this being a topic of our utmost concern, most of the discussion centered on strategizing how landowners might stand to make more money, limit their liability, and understand crop production levels if they do in fact allow an easement to lay pipe on their lands to hold pressurized carbon dioxide. Very little conversation covered the potential dangers to human life, water, land, plant, and animal relatives.

We learned about how the project proposes to lay two thousand miles of pipe across our area and the five states of *Mni Sota*, North and South Dakota, Iowa, and Nebraska. The project intends to capture carbon and cash through the 2021 Infrastructure Investment and Jobs Act. There's a lot of money to be made by corporations and individual investors using many of the time-tested shenanigans, including breaking the project into multiple jurisdictions, stages, and phases to gain carbon sequestration credits. Yet, the most insidious part of the deal is that it's a false solution, promoted as a response to climate change. I wonder about the increased carbon emissions through the processes involved in the capturing of carbon from ethanol plants and refineries (distilling, compressing, chilling, and liquefying the carbon before moving it into pipelines); making, shipping, and installing pipe; and storing the carbon dioxide in deep geological locations. All phases would potentially put water, soils, animals, and humans in harm's way. Carbon pipelines have yet to be proved effective, but still, according to the Indigenous-led Great Plains Action Society, the $4.5 billion investment in the "Midwest Carbon Express" is plowing forward. That is, unless we pull together to fight the good fight. Today, I brought some words to our gathering to add to our joint op-ed piece we're writing in an attempt to call others into the fight. As we noshed on *paśdayapi*, zucchini bread, and apple pie, I thought about the ingredients grown in and harvested from this land. Each of us has the right to clean water, land, and air. How and in what way will you fight the good fight?

RECONCILING

I probably can count the number of times Jay and I have had a "fight." During these conflicts, I typically step outside to blow off steam. Several years ago, my faithful dad and his chainsaw skills helped us clear a spot along the slope of our land to take in the beauty of Mni Oḣdoka Taŋka. He has cut wood to heat his home most of his life and still does even into his elder years. In no time, they cleared the space, and Jay built me a bench and rolled a big log next to it for a footrest. Cedar boughs hang on each side of the vista, along with the cumbersome and invasive buckthorn. Black birds caw, squirrels chatter, and hawks and eagles screech overhead while listening to the year-round babbling creek below. We call this space our "zen spot." Here is where Jay will join me after some time to make up. It is in this spot that perspective emerges, and tender relationships are all that matter. It is interesting how we seek outdoor spaces to gain changed viewpoints.

Perhaps twenty years ago, when my children were young and I was actively learning to speak the Dakota language, I asked Kuŋši about the word *išnati*. Grandma replied, "Oh, you are talking about long time ago." It is a time when Dakota women would isolate from the rest of their family and people during their moon time. The girls and women would work on their handicrafts and enjoy one another's company while being fed and cared for. This was a reprieve from the daily toils of cooking and caring for others and occurred naturally every month. Can you imagine if women practiced this today, how rested, balanced, and sane we would be? I decided to experiment with my own personal *išnati* by renting a house in the country just thirty miles north of our then home in town. I decided that during my inaugural *išnati*, I would work through processing some traumas and the emotional pain I worked hard to bury. Well into the deep work, my weeping indoors just seemed stifling. So, I escaped to the outdoors, to the largest tree, one I would equate to a grandmother tree. At least that is how she seemed to me. As the wind picked up, seemingly mirroring my anguish and carrying it all away, I cried and wailed for some time. While I clung to the tree, her branches seemed to embrace me, giving me much-needed comfort. I was so grateful to have had the privacy to free myself from that pent-up baggage.

Oak tree in our backyard. Photograph by Tanner Peterson.

Today, I believe that grandmother tree was a highly connected hub tree, or what is fondly called a *mother tree*. Mother trees truly live up to their name. They share excess carbon and nitrogen with other trees, saplings, and plants, yet favor their own kin. Along their root systems, mycorrhizal fungi live in cooperative relationship. The symbiosis was through the sharing and transporting of carbon and information. Mycorrhizal fungi also help break down organic matter, thus stabilizing soils, an important role in carbon sequestration. In other words, this weblike string of connections helps plants and trees gain access to soil nutrients and water. There is a lot of research today on fungi and their many benefits to cleaning up toxins and their uses in land restoration practices. For example, studies are underway on the use of arbuscular mycorrhizal fungi as a counter to fertilizers in agriculture where the network of mycelium promotes nutrient uptake. Scientists and researchers are discovering the wisdom of our plant relatives. They are living and communicating through deep relationships, alliances, and kinship networks. And yes, I do believe the grandmother tree sensed my distress and offered me comfort and solace. I released my toxic pain and emotions by expelling carbon dioxide from my wailing mouth and salty tears that were in turn received by the grandmother tree.

I hold many of these memories, images, and sensations of how Mother Earth and all her creation have taken care of me. Daily escapes from the living room or office, with worry or anxiety, have been exchanged for refuge outside on our back deck. I will shake my hands, arms, and body to release tension and reregulate. I took up this practice after learning about how many animals, including dogs, ducks, and bears, shake or flap to release stress. They do this and then move on, or they do it to simply wake up the body. After some shaking in the privacy of my back deck, I will do a few yoga stretches and take fresh outdoor breath into my belly. The deck is also the place where I gaze up into the night sky and watch the countless stars. The Covid-19 pandemic, a relative's death, news of an impending World War III, a son in jail, and more fear-jarring events and situations completely out of my control have been

released to the star nation and to Grandmother Moon. The land
and all that our Mother holds have been my place of solace, recov-
ery, rebalancing, and comfort. She provides space to grieve, seek
understanding, and resolve problems. I love listening to the music
of Michael Franti and Spearhead. In their song "Good Day for a
Good Day," they express so simply and clearly what I believe—
that we are all connected and we're all trying to heal: "Everybody
was born to a Momma / Everybody's trynna heal like trauma."
Whether perceived or real, the land, plant, and animal life, water,
and outdoor air have indeed cradled much of my conflict.

During a work training on conflict and the practice of being a
good relative, we were asked to reflect on our early lessons around
conflict. I hold many positive memories from my childhood, including church life. Yet in hindsight, I can see now that a strict
religious and sheltered upbringing did not provide me with adequate tools to effectively navigate conflict. Obedience without
questioning was rewarded, and expressing conflict was seen
as disrupting the peace. As I reflect on this, my mind jumps to
a recent visit to a friend's home. I was observing how they were
straightening and ensuring alignment of the kitchen towels and
tidying up to perfection. Curious, I commented on their behavior.
Not only did they acknowledge it, but they also explained how it
was one aspect of their life they could exercise control over. Perhaps the same was true for my dad, a military veteran. He may
have found security in stringent structures and rigidity as he
navigated his own childhood challenges. One of the refreshing
components of this training was not to lay blame but to bring
awareness and incorporate some tools for dealing with conflict,
because, honestly, it is everywhere. We were asked to share what
skills we gained from early lessons around conflict that we could
bring forward to honor being a good relative to ourselves. This
prompt caused me to move from a raised heart rate and anxiety to
a release of breath and an emerging smile. I love my parents and
am grateful for all that they have taught me. One gift I have gained
despite rewarded silence and the avoidance of expressing conflict
is acute observation. I am keenly aware when there is underlying

conflict. I pick up on slight body movements, subtle facial expressions, and change in energies. The trainer shared that we do not just eliminate what has been perhaps engrained over decades, but we can increase our awareness of default behaviors, exercise compassion and understanding for ourselves and others, and create room for discussion and democratic collective decision-making—emphasizing that relationships are everything.

As I write this, snow is still on the ground, yet I know in a few weeks Jay will start tapping trees outdoors and I will start some seedlings indoors. The gardens have been my place in between all the words, meetings, and work projects, the place where I am able to clear my brain, work through problems, and gain creative and sometimes just simple solutions. Conflict, whether perceived, anticipated, or all-out real—Mother Earth, her waters, the flora and fauna continue to take care of me. *Ina Maka kiŋ awaŋuŋhdakapi heoŋ toked he awaŋyake waśkaŋ he?* Mother Earth takes care of us. How will I take care of her?

In my spring season, I memorized, played, and sang
    Liturgy from L-C-A, E-L-C-A, and L-C-M-S.
    I followed the rows, observant as a wallflower, gathering
        canons along the way.
The summer season arrived so quickly and oh what a busy summer
  season it was!
    Together now, we lit a candle in unity at our own L-C-M-S,
    And it was so beautiful what we planted.
    But that's when all that searching and scratching began.
    An arduous journey of belongingness and perhaps a reliving
      of springtime innocence?
    Uncontented all summer, I searched the rows of pews.
    U-C-C, P-C, C-M-A, E-L-C-A, L-C-M-C.
Then it happened, suddenly, or so it seemed.
The days became shorter and the evenings closer.
That autumn wind brought waves where the should-haves and
  ought-tos were pulled out to sea.
    Unbounded from fences and walls of doctrine, in the daybreak
      liberated and freed.
It was the time when the moon is known for shaking off leaves
    That I stopped searching for steepled buildings,
    And that seasonal wind revealed my knowing and bare tree.
No longer riddled with guilt, nor thirsty for quest
    Because I knew then, the almighty architect is with me to
      commune at no rest.
Now late in this season, I am left in adulation
    Of geese, the hummingbirds, and the red-winged blackbirds
      in their outbound flights,
        And sing and forage with northern cardinals, pheasants,
        and the red-bellied woodpeckers.
For the star Polaris is now in sight, and the shift in my axis is just
  beginning to tilt.
The communion now quickened from daily to tick, as the marrow
  within slowly recedes
    And finally, now I am—still.

Lessons and Gifts
to Consider and Cultivate

▲▲▲

I believe most people are inherently good and that collectively we hold the solutions to our greatest challenges. Gabor Maté, in *The Myth of Normal*, describes our greatest challenge as "the disconnection from ourselves, from one another, and from the planet." We only need to watch the news or scan our community and familial spaces to feel the monumental and despairing consequences of that disconnection. In my office, I have a poster that reminds me of possibility. It is titled "Seven Core Assumptions: What We Believe to Be True" and is produced by Living Justice Press; the poster acknowledges assumptions that were derived from Indigenous teachings. Here are a few that resonate with me the most: "The true self in everyone is good, wise, and powerful. The world is profoundly connected. Everything we need to make positive change is already here." I trust that we as human beings will find our way to practice and live in more sustainable and balanced ways and be in right relationship with all that is. To believe otherwise is to relinquish hope and forgo all I have been taught from our Dakota ways of knowing and being. My everyday thoughts and practices as a gardener, a lover of the land, a fellow human being, and relative originate as gifts and lessons from ancestors, relatives, allies, and mentors. To honor and reciprocate, I offer up this collection of writings in hope that we each find our ceremony to renew a spirit of connectedness and oneness. There are also number of resources provided in the "Further Reading and Resources" section to draw from. I invite you, a fellow relative, to sit quietly under a tree or near a waterway, in a park, or in your garden and consider the following principles and reflective questions.

Makoce kiŋ he Dakota makocetawapi ye. **This land is Indigenous homeland.**

A long-overdue movement is under way that acknowledges that our nation is founded on the theft of Indigenous land. And yet words alone do not necessarily lead to action. We need to move beyond land acknowledgment statements and ask *What will be different?* Beyond Land Acknowledgement, an educational online series produced by the Native Governance Center in Minnesota, provides support to move beyond "another form of optical allyship." Examples of solidarity would include institutions and organizations whose land acknowledgment statement serves as a starting point and foundation to truth telling, healing, and restorative action.

Makoce kiŋ dena Dakota makoce tawapi ye. These lands are Indigenous homelands.

Whose land are you living on—what Indigenous peoples call the lands you stand on their original homelands? How might you give honor to those Indigenous people and lands you reside on? Equally important, what plants and animals are indigenous to the land you call home? How can we, too, ensure their livelihood?

Makoce kiŋ mitakuye. The land is my relative.

Yankton Dakota scholar Zitkala-Ša, also known as Gertrude Bonnin, was an early advocate for justice and self-determination for American Indians. Her writing reflects the gap and bridging between two worldviews she experienced. In the essay "The Great Spirit," Zitkala-Ša demonstrates the healing and nurturing space of nature and finding solace while being out on the land, "My heart and I lie small upon the earth like a grain of throbbing sand. Drifting clouds and tinkling waters, together . . . the loving Mystery round about us." How can one not sense the loving embrace of Mother Earth while lying upon her, or feel the healing powers of water?

Makoce kiŋ mitakuye. The land is my relative.
 In what ways do you honor and treat the land as a relative? What are some of the ways you are reclaiming a relationship with the land?

Ina Maka kiŋ awaŋuŋhdakapi heoŋ toked he awaŋyake waśkaŋ he? Mother Earth takes care of us—how will I take care of her?
 Beloved writer Robin Wall Kimmerer, Citizen Potawatomi Nation, folds together science and Indigenous wisdom in her book *Braiding Sweetgrass.* Like a great storyteller, she weaves in lessons on and examples of being a good relative to Mother Earth—from prayer, gifting, and exercising resourcefulness to land restoration.
 What are some activities or practices you do that demonstrate care and appreciation for Mother Earth? What new practice might you adopt that honors this understanding and relationship?

Anokataŋhaŋ kicicuwapi. **Reciprocity.**
 Anokataŋhaŋ kicicuwapi. Mitakuye owasiŋ. Reciprocity. All My Relations.
 I just love it when you find someone who speaks exactly what your heart and spirit have felt. I cry, I laugh, I hold my breath, my heart swells, and everything in between as I read the poems of Mary Oliver, the late gifted writer and Pulitzer Prize–winning poet. Oliver understood and so beautifully expressed the interconnectedness between us and everything. For example, in her book *Upstream: Selected Essays,* she writes, "The farthest star and

the mud at our feet are a family." And her words compel us to recognize and act according to this understanding of relationality: "we are at risk together, or we are on our way to a sustainable world together."

How do we shift our individualistic and arrogant mindset to one that understands we are all connected? What actions or behaviors change as a result of embracing reciprocity?

Wicoicaǧe. Yuhepica. **Generational. Sustainable.**

Joy Harjo, Muscogee Creek, who served three terms as our nation's poet laureate, advises us to remember the Indigenous peoples of the land we reside on and to respect all of creation—whether people, plant, or animal. I especially love these words in her book *Conflict for Holy Beings*: "The land is a being who remembers everything. You will have to answer to your children, and their children, and theirs."

Wicoicaǧe. Yuhepica. Generational. Sustainable.

What tradition are you maintaining and passing on to future generations—perhaps a family practice that supports sustainability? What new attitude or practice could you adopt that upholds the value of sustainability?

Further Reading and Resources

BOOKS

Brendtro, Larry K., Martin Brokenleg, and Steve Van Bockern. *Reclaiming Youth at Risk: Futures of Promise.* 2nd ed. Bloomington, Ind: Solution Tree Press, 2002.

Brown, Adrienne Maree. *Emergent Strategy: Shaping Change, Changing Worlds.* Chico, Calif.: AK Press, 2017.

Butler, Octavia E. *Parable of the Sower.* New York: Grand Central Publishing, 2023.

Deloria, Ella Cara. *Waterlily.* Lincoln: University of Nebraska Press, 2009.

Dominguez, S. R. *American Indian Stories.* Lincoln: University of Nebraska Press, 2003.

Durand, Paul. *Where the Waters Gather and the Rivers Meet: An Atlas of the Eastern Sioux.* Faribault, Minn.: Paul Durand, 1994.

Eastman, Charles Alexander, and Elaine Goodale Eastman. *Wigwam Evenings: Sioux Folk Tales Retold.* Boston: Little, Brown, 1909.

Harjo, Joy. *Conflict Resolution for Holy Beings: Poems.* New York: W. W. Norton, 2015.

Kimmerer, Robin Wall. *Braiding Sweetgrass: Indigenous Wisdom, Scientific Knowledge, and the Teachings of Plants.* Minneapolis: Milkweed Editions, 2013.

Maté, Gabor. *The Myth of Normal: Trauma, Illness & Healing in a Toxic Culture.* New York: Avery, 2022.

Mock, Sarah K. *Farm (and Other F Words): The Rise and Fall of Small Family Farms.* Potomac, Md.: New Degree Press, 2021.

Oliver, Mary. *Devotions: The Selected Poems of Mary Oliver.* New York: Penguin, 2017.

Oliver, Mary. *Upstream: Selected Essays.* New York: Penguin, 2019.

Peterson, Teresa R., and Walter LaBatte Jr. *Voices from Pejuhutazizi: Dakota Stories and Storytellers.* St. Paul: Minnesota Historical Society Press, 2022.

Schaefer, Carol. *Grandmothers Counsel the World: Women Elders Offer Their Vision for Our Planet.* Boston: Trumpeter Books, 2006.

Spector, Janet. *What This Awl Means.* St. Paul: Minnesota Historical Society Press, 2009.

Upham, Warren. *Minnesota Place Names: Geographical Encyclopedia.* 3rd ed. St. Paul: Minnesota Historical Society Press, 2001.

Westerman, Gwen, and Bruce M. White. *Mni Sota Makoce: The Land of the Dakota.* St. Paul: Minnesota Historical Society Press, 2012.

Wilson, Diane. *The Seed Keeper.* Minneapolis: Milkweed Editions, 2021.

Wilson, Gilbert Livingstone. *Buffalo Bird Woman's Garden: Agriculture of the Hidatsa Indians.* St. Paul: Minnesota Historical Society Press, 1987.

Wilson, Shawn. *Research Is Ceremony: Indigenous Research Methods.* Black Point, Nova Scotia: Fernwood Publishing, 2008.

ORGANIZATIONS

Agriculture Drainage Management Coalition https://admcoalition.com

Blue Thumb—Planting for Clean Water https://bluethumb.org

Clean Up the River Environment https://curemn.org

Dakota Wicohan https://dakotawicohan.org

Dream of Wild Health https://dreamofwildhealth.org

Emergence Magazine https://emergencemagazine.org

Great Plains Action Society https://www.greatplainsaction.org

Minnesota Center for Environmental Advocacy https://www.mncenter.org

Minnesota Historical Society—Dakota People https://www.mnhs.org/fortsnelling/learn/native-americans/dakota-people

National Native American Boarding School Healing Coalition https://boardingschoolhealing.org

National Pesticide Information Center http://npic.orst.edu

Native American Food Sovereignty Alliance https://nativefoodalliance.org

Native Governance Center https://nativegov.org
Pollinator Partnership https://www.pollinator.org
Seed Savers Exchange https://seedsavers.org
U.S. Environmental Protection Agency https://www.epa.gov
U.S. Fish and Wildlife Service—Status and Trends of Prairie
  Wetlands in the United States https://www.fws.gov/wetlands
  /documents/Status-and-Trends-of-Prairie-Wetlands-in-the
  -United-States-1997-to-2009.pdf

Acknowledgments

Wopida taŋka eciciyapi!

My deepest gratitude goes to so many who provided gifts and lessons to me—shaping who I am and showing me how to be a good relative.

To my ma and dad—I can't imagine how different life would be today had I not experienced life on the farm. I'm forever grateful for all that you have taught me.

To so many relatives and teachers along the way, including those who have now gone on to the spirit world. Some of their gifts and lessons are included in the telling throughout this book, but there are too many names to mention. My hope is that in my sharing I am reciprocating in a way that honors them.

To Mona Susan Power, who shared her stories and gave inspiration and encouragement during her incredibly gracious developmental edit review. To the gracious readers who gave feedback and asked good questions to further the development of the writing—Janet Maylen, Paul Dearhouse, Mary Peters, Patrick Moore, Diane Wilson, Marie Zimmerman, and Heather Peters. To my early Native Women's Writing Group, led by author and mentor Diane Wilson, who offered me the encouragement to keep on writing.

To the Minnesota State Arts Board, for the Creative Support for Individuals grant that provided time, space, and support for writing retreats.

To Dekśi Super and Icepaŋśi Raine, both of whom provided guidance on *Dakota Iapi.*

And to Erik Anderson, who enthusiastically believed in this book, and the talented team at the University of Minnesota Press, including Mary Byers, who made editing enjoyable: my appreciation for passing along the gifts and lessons to all who will listen.

TERESA PETERSON, *Utuhu Cistiŋna Wiŋ*, is Sisseton Wahpeton Dakota and citizen of the Upper Sioux Community. She is author of the children's book *Grasshopper Girl* and of *Voices from Pejuhutazizi: Dakota Stories and Storytellers*, cowritten with her uncle, Walter LaBatte Jr. She has a doctorate degree in education from the University of Minnesota Duluth and is program manager for the foundation at NDN Collective. Her passions are digging in her garden that overlooks the Mni Sota River valley and feeding friends and family.